# THE
# BALLINAMORE AND BALLYCONNELL CANAL

# INLAND WATERWAYS HISTORIES

### Edited by Charles Hadfield

# THE BALLINAMORE
# AND BALLYCONNELL
# CANAL

by

## PATRICK FLANAGAN

DAVID & CHARLES: NEWTON ABBOT

ISBN 0 7153 5613 5

Set in 11 pt Garamond, 2 pt leaded
and printed in Great Britain
by Latimer Trend & Company Limited Plymouth
for David & Charles (Publishers) Limited
South Devon House   Newton Abbot   Devon

# Contents

# Illustrations

9

Many years ago there was a Ballinamore canal . . . It was
the finest canal that was built in Britain up to that time . . .
*Major Harry Lefroy, 1923*

It is one of the most shameful pieces of mismanagement in
any country—not in Turkey could there be such a piece of
mismanagement as that Ballinamore Canal.
*John Grey Vesey Porter, 1881*

# CHAPTER 1

# The Background

In all your life have you ever seen a country so dead
and stagnant . . . as the County Leitrim?

*J. G. V. Porter, 1881*

THE Ballinamore & Ballyconnell Navigation, more frequently
referred to simply as the Ballinamore Canal, is an interesting
mixture of still-water canal and river navigation which has
some fair-sized lakes along its course for good measure. It was
built primarily to link two of the more important Irish rivers—
the Erne, which flows roughly north-west through Cavan and
Fermanagh to the Atlantic at Ballyshannon, in south Donegal,
and the Shannon, which rises in County Cavan and flows south
for over 100 miles to the sea at Limerick. By the 1840s, when
the scheme for the Ballinamore canal was conceived and implemented, the development of the principal inland navigations
of Ireland was virtually complete. From the Erne it was possible to reach Belfast and Newry by water, while the Shannon
was doubly linked to Dublin, via the midlands, by the Royal
and Grand canals. Thus the completion of this link of forty-
odd miles would unify the waterway network very nicely.

Of the 38 miles of the Ballinamore Canal, some 5 consist of
a still-water navigation, 8 lie through lakes and the rest com-
prise the canalised courses of the Yellow and Woodford rivers.
About 22 miles lie wholly in Leitrim, 8 in Cavan and the rest
form either the Cavan/Leitrim or Cavan/Fermanagh boundary.
The latter is the case for the first 6½ miles of the navigation
from Lough Erne. Commencing at a point about 4 miles north

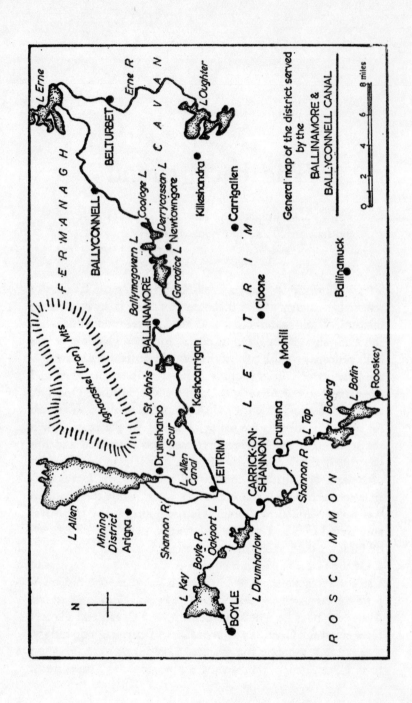

General map of the district served
by the
**BALLINAMORE &
BALLYCONNELL CANAL**

0   2   4   6   8 miles

of the town of Belturbet the navigation runs south-west for 3 miles to Aghalane, where it turns to head north-west for 2 miles. Beyond Caroul it resumes its south-westerly course and after 3 miles passes the town of Ballyconnell. Five miles further on the waterway enters a chain of lakes—Coologe, Derrycassan and Ballymagovern—flowing in a rather more westerly direction. Leaving Ballymagovern Lake it passes Woodford Demesne and enters Garadice Lake, the largest on the system with an area of some 1,100 acres. This far the route has been along the course of the Woodford River which, west of Garadice Lake, becomes the Yellow River. Although the western outfall of Garadice Lake is only 3 miles from Ballinamore the canal takes a U-shaped course of some 4½ miles to reach the town.

Heading north out of Ballinamore the canal soon turns west and runs along the course of the Yellow River to Creevy, a distance of about 2 miles. Here the navigation turns south-west again and, following a new channel, comes to St John's Lake about a mile further on. This 'lake' is in fact a series of three small lakes and the navigation threads southwards through them to Muckros where it diverges west for 1½ miles along the old course of the Aghacashlaun River to Castlefore. Again the waterway heads south-west, along what is virtually a new cut, through Lough Marrave, into Lough Scur. From this lake, which is the central point of the summit level, the navigation runs south-west for some 5 miles to the Shannon, just beyond Leitrim village. This last section is virtually a pure still-water canal, although near Leitrim the Black Lough and the Leitrim River were incorporated into its course.

The region through which the canal flows is characterised by a great number of small lakes and low hills, although there is some high ground to the north of its course. Ballyconnell lies at the foot of 'the bleak, barren and lofty range of the Slieve Russell mountains' while the canal is fed by the rivers rushing down from the range of the Aghacashel Mountains, the principal peaks of which are Slieve Anierin (1,922ft), Slievenakilla

(1,793ft), Gubnaveagh (1,707ft) and Benbrack (1,648ft). Two of the rivers flow into Lough Scur and one into St John's Lough. The land served by the canal is poor and nowadays very sparsely inhabited, the population being little more than a quarter of what it was a century ago. Ballinamore and Ballyconnell are the only significant towns along the canal, though by any standards they could never have been considered large. The latter had a population of around 400 in the 1840s but Ballinamore was rather larger and was distinguished by its important market and its 'remarkably clean, airy, comfortable and prosperous appearance'. Two other small towns lie on or near the canal—Keshcarrigan, near Castlefore, described in 1846 as a 'poor, squalid place', and Leitrim village, of which it was remarked at that time too that it was 'so unpeopled and deserted, that scarce one remains there to tell anything about it'.

This was hardly promising country for a canal and were it not for the benefits expected from a Shannon–Erne link it would never have been built. As things turned out this would, perhaps, have been just as well for the canal was destined to remain virtually unused and to spend most of its lifetime quietly decaying. Various factors contributed to the birth of the Ballinamore Canal, all of them culminating in the proceedings of the mid-1840s. However, there had been much earlier suggestions for a navigation of a very similar nature. To follow the growth of early interest in the project it is necessary to consider briefly the background to the spread of inland waterways in Ireland.

The first petition to have the Shannon made navigable from County Leitrim to Limerick was made in 1697 and twelve years later there was a second such request to the government.[1] Action was taken in 1715 when the first Irish inland navigation Act was passed. In the ensuing half-century many schemes were projected and quite a number actually brought to the construction stage. Work on the Shannon itself began in the 1750s after the 'Corporation for Promoting and Carrying on an Inland Navigation in Ireland' had been established in 1751. Two de-

cades later work began on the Grand Canal and the first main
arteries of the Irish canal system started to grow. By then there
had been significant developments in the north-east, too, and
towards the end of the 1770s interest awakened in the north-
west. The canal engineer, Richard Evans, developed a plan for
quite an extensive navigation and parliamentary approval was
granted in 1778.[2]

Starting from a sea terminal at Murray's Quay in Ballyshannon, a canal would run close to the unnavigable Erne for some
5 miles to Belleek. Past the falls above Belleek, the canal would
enter Lower Lough Erne, through which lake a navigable
channel would be made to Enniskillen. From there the navigation would continue through Upper Lough Erne to Belturbet.
Short of that town there would be a branch navigation along
the Woodford River to Ballyconnell. It was envisaged at the
time that a future extension would be to Ballinamore, Lough
Scur and the Shannon at Leitrim.

Work on the scheme commenced in 1780 and in subsequent
years men were at work in places along part of the route of the
later Ballinamore Canal. The course of this navigation was laid
out by Evans, who also made the necessary arrangements with
the contractors. Progress was none too smooth, for in 1783 the
people in the region petitioned the Irish parliament for aid. The
move resulted in a grant of £1,000, but a second petition for
assistance made in 1785 merely resulted in Evans being called
on to make an inspection and to report on how the £1,000 had
been spent.[3] That was in 1786 and, despite Evans's report of
definite progress, no more aid was forthcoming and work
stopped. Quite an amount of work had been done—a lock was
more than half built at Caroul, and materials made ready for its
completion, and a lock house had been built. Even the lock
gates had been made, 'of excellent materials', but to no avail—
all works had been stopped by 1792.

In April 1793 came a report from another engineer, William
Chapman of Newcastle, 'On the means of making Woodford
River navigable from Lough-Erne to Woodford-Lough',

B

# ESTIMATE

## OF THE EXPENCE

## OF A PROPOSED NAVIGATION,

### From *LOUGH ERNE*

### To *WOODFORD LOUGH.*

---

|  | £. | s. | d. |
|---|---|---|---|
| Four Locks of 63 feet between the Gates, 12½ width of chamber and of various falls, at £.350 | 1400 | 0 | 0 |
| Bridges over the Locks at Aughaline and Ballyheady, - - | 120 | 0 | 0 |
| Removing the Bar below Mullinacough and two shoals below Aughaline-bridge, - - | 150 | 0 | 0 |
| Deepening the shoals at Kilcorby and at the Eel Weir at Curhoul, | 80 | 0 | 0 |
| Finishing the Canal and Weir at Curhoul, - - - | 270 | 0 | 0 |
| Making a Channel within the Island opposite Annagh Wood, and removing all obstructions to as far as the great Island below Ballyconnel, | 75 | 0 | 0 |
| Five miles of Trackway from the junction of Woodford River with the Erne, 2 miles of which I suppose high enough, and the rest to average 2 feet height, which with sodding may amount to 4s. 8d. per Perch, or 74l. 13s. 4d. per Mile, | 224 | 0 | 0 |

Canal

|  | £. | s. | d. |
|---|---|---|---|
| Canal above and below the Lock at Ballyconnel Mills, - | 110 | 0 | 0 |
| Deepening the Mill-course and repairing the Weir, - | 80 | 0 | 0 |
| Deepening and contracting the shallow parts of the River between Ballyconnel and Ballyheady, about | 400 | 0 | 0 |
| 600 Perches of Trackway, at an average of 5s. per, - | 150 | 0 | 0 |
| Canal at Ballyheady and alterations of the Weir, - - - | 140 | 0 | 0 |
| Deepening and contracting various parts of the River between Ballyheady and Curleach, - | 160 | 0 | 0 |
| 500 Perches of Trackway, at 5s. per, | 125 | 0 | 0 |
| Canal at Curleach, - - | 90 | 0 | 0 |
| Towing Paths on the communications between the Loughs of Curleach, Burren, Ballymagauran and Woodford, about 200 Perches, at an average of 10s. per Perch, | 100 | 0 | 0 |
| Making a deep channel through the Eel Weir below Mr. Gore's, deepening the channel into Woodford Lough, and making a Navigation Arch in the Bridge, - | 250 | 0 | 0 |
| Boats and Machinery, - | 150 | 0 | 0 |
|  | 4374 | 0 | 0 |
| Incidents and Superintendance, 15 per Cent. | 655 | 7 | 0 |
|  | £.5029 | 7 | 0 |

*F I N I S.*

FIG 1. William Chapman's estimate of 1793

which dealt with the proposed navigation very fully.[4] In Chapman's view there were no insurmountable difficulties and for £5,000 a navigation would be made from Woodford (Garadice) Lough to Lough Erne. The principal features of his proposed navigation were locks at 'the rapids at Curhoul' (Caroul, where a lock was already near completion), at Ballyconnell, at Ballyheady Bridge, at the outfall of Coologe Lough (in the vicinity of Skelan Ford), and at Aghalane Bridge. New bridges were recommended at Aghalane and Ballyheady locks and Chapman proposed that expediture at Ballyconnell be reduced by making use of the head-race for the mill instead of following the river course proper. He thought that the navigation should be capable of handling boats from 10 to 20 tons, drawing 2–2½ft in summer and up to 4ft of water in winter. For haulage he felt that a 'narrow path for men' would suffice, as there would be much difficulty in providing a horse towing path because neither side of the river was 'favourable for a track-way for the whole length'.

It is a little difficult to understand Chapman's recommendation that the navigation be extended as far west as Garadice Lake, for there could have been little hope of any worthwhile traffic from the few scattered hamlets in the region. However, he was certainly aware of the possibility of an extension westwards towards the Shannon, for he spelt out the details. From Garadice it was over 4 miles to Ballinamore, though this could be cut by a mile if a canal were built. From Ballinamore it was

> just two miles further to the outlet of the Lough of Ballyduff, from whence it is Navigable by a chain of small Lakes to the west end of the Lough north of Kishcarrigan; from which, a Canal of about four miles in length, would pass through favourable ground in the vale north of Sheebeg, and onwards to the Shannon at Leitrim.[5]

In other words he mapped out fairly closely the course of the navigation made a half-century later. In one respect, however, Chapman was more than a little wide of the mark in his prediction

Not having ascertained the quantity of rise and fall in this line,
I can't take upon myself to say further, than that the expense
will be moderate, compared both with the distance and the
object.[6]

Chapman ended his comments on the possibility of extension
with a brief discussion of the feasibility of bringing smaller
boats within different distances of Ballinamore by doing the
minimum of work, advancing the opinion that if anything were
to be done by way of an extension it should be by canal to
Ballyduff, rather than by river course. He thought that the
possibility of the link with the Shannon would stimulate practical interest in the Woodford–Lough Erne navigation, but he
was convinced that the scheme then in hand could not proceed
unless the Ballyshannon–Belleek link were completed.

In the preceding years work had also been done on this latter
canal; earthworks had been carried out and one lock, of a projected twelve, was built near Belleek.[7] But in 1794 funds ran
out; the scheme expired and with it died the Woodford River
project. An attempt was made to revive the works in 1801,
when the newly-established Directors-General of Inland Navigation asked Evans to submit a revised estimate. His reply was
that the original sum of £40,000—for the combined navigations
—should be increased to £48,000 but once again no funds were
forthcoming and the plans were dropped, the partly completed
works being abandoned for good. It was nearly 40 years later
before any further detailed attention was given to the Woodford
River.

# CHAPTER 2

# Vital Legislation

I think, that viewing the subject generally, no doubt can be entertained of its remunerative nature, and especially when it is considered as the means of connecting nearly all the Inland Navigations of Ireland.

*W. T. Mulvany, 1839*

THE dawn of the nineteenth century saw some important changes which had a bearing both on the country in general and on inland navigation in particular. The Act of Union of 1800 spelt the end of the Irish parliament which had made the grant towards the Woodford navigation in 1783 and henceforth all Acts concerning Irish waterways would originate in London. In 1800, too, the Directors-General of Inland Navigation were established and given control of most of the Irish navigations. This body of course concerned itself with the Shannon and paid some—though unfortunately not enough —attention to the terminal canals at either end of the Shannon river navigation, which connected it to Lough Allen and to the sea at Limerick. But the directors-general were not concerned about any Shannon–Erne link and many years passed before the subject was raised again.

In 1831 the Commissioners of Public Works in Ireland were appointed and among the powers entrusted to them were those of the directors-general.[1] This new body, almost invariably referred to as the Board of Works (BOW), was later to play the leading role in the early history of the Ballinamore canal. In the same year a commission was appointed to investigate the Shannon navigation and in 1834 a select committee of the

22

House of Commons began to consider the same topic.[2] The first Shannon Navigation Act was passed in 1835 and more commissioners were appointed, charged with the duty of preparing plans and surveys for the improvement of the Shannon. After four years the preliminaries were completed and, by the Shannon Navigation Act of 1839, the 'Shannon Commissioners' were appointed to undertake extensive works estimated to cost £584,806. Their task was to take over a decade; it was not until 1852 that the commissioners handed over their responsibilities to the BOW, which body had been given legal responsibility for the Shannon in 1846.

The question of a Shannon–Erne link was not overlooked in all the planning for the improvement of the Shannon itself. The preparatory commission of 1835 raised the topic, after a reference had been made to it by the Treasury. William T. Mulvany, a civil engineer in the employ of the commission, was instructed to report on the practicability of making such a link and was required to examine the terrain between the Shannon at Drumsna and the Erne at Belturbet or 'the point near Wattle Bridge, where the Ulster Canal is to open into the River Erne'.[3] The Ulster Canal Company had itself financed surveys of more or less the same territory in 1837–8 with a view to the future extension of its navigation, and possibly the Treasury's interest had been stimulated by that company.

Mulvany's report was dated 11 March 1839 and it stated that he had

> perambulated the whole line of summit southwards through the County of Leitrim into the County of Longford, where it terminates in the high hills south east of Ballinamuck.[4]

The terrain, although not mountainous in general, was dotted with hills and Mulvany was primarily concerned with finding a suitable summit level for a canal. He came up with three possibilities—the passes at Letterfine near Lough Scur, leading to Ballinamore (which he termed 'the Ballinamore Line'); at Fort Lough between Mohill and Carrigallen ('the Mohill Line'); and at Cloncoose Lough near Ballinamuck ('the Ballinamuck Line').

He ruled out the Mohill line on the grounds of expense and inadequacy of water supply. Some 20 locks would be required and a heavy cutting would have to be made at the summit level. The route ran from near Drumsna through Mohill town, on to the north of Cloone, to Killygar and into the Erne at Killeshandra. All in all, Mulvany was not impressed with the route and, indeed, he examined it mainly because a trial section of it had been made by the Ulster Canal Company which seemed to think it would be the most advantageous one commercially.

The Ballinamuck line was likewise ruled out by Mulvany for various reasons. For the first 16 miles of its length the route lay through boggy country which could have yielded nothing in the way of traffic; there could be competition from the relatively close Royal Canal, a branch of which served Longford; and, not least important, the summit level was very low. This would have resulted in a saving in locks—he thought 10 or 11 would suffice—but would also have posed great problems of water supply. The line ran from the Shannon at Lough Forbes along the Leitrim/Longford boundary to Killeshandra and the Erne.

Both these lines stopped 14 miles short of the ultimate goal —Belturbet—and the navigation would continue by Lough Oughter and the Erne from Killeshandra to that town. This stretch was a natural navigation and had sufficient depth for boats almost the whole way. At Belturbet, however, there was a fall of some 8 feet and to overcome this obstacle Mulvany proposed that a lock, 110ft by 25ft, and a weir be built 'near the distillery above the bridge' and that some deepening be carried out below the bridge. From there onwards there was again an adequate natural navigation for the 7 miles to Wattle Bridge, the chosen western terminus of the Ulster Canal.

The third possibility, and the one favoured by Mulvany, was the Ballinamore line, on which the summit level was the most favourable. It was at 220ft OD, necessitating about 15 locks, and its catchment was such, in Mulvany's opinion, as to provide an adequate water supply 'without the construction of supply-

Showing the relative CAPABILITIES (in an Engineering point of view) of the several Lines, examined for the purposes of a proposed JUNCTION CANAL, between the RIVERS SHANNON and ERNE.

| Description of Line. | Length in Statute Miles. | Height of proposed Summit Level above the Sea. (Feet.) | Total Rise and Fall. (Feet.) | Deepest Cutting at Summit. (Ft. In.) | Rate of Lockage per Statute Mile. (Ft.Dec.) | No. of Locks required. | Area of Catchment Basin for supply of Summit Level. (Statute Acres.) | Observations. |
|---|---|---|---|---|---|---|---|---|
| The Ballinamore Line, { Canal, 28¼ ; River, 1 } | 29¼ | 220 | 150 | 23  0 | 5.00 | 16 | 10,320, including 670 of Lakes, - | See Fig. No. 1, Sheet of Sections. |
| Do., by Killeshandra, { Canal, 24½ ; River & Lake, 14 } | 38½ | 220½ | 150 | Do. | 5.75* | 16 | Do.   Do. | Do.   Do. |
| The Mohill Line, (examined by the Ulster Canal Company.) | 30 | 239 | 196 | 31  6 | 6.53 | 21 | 970, including 48 acres of Lakes. - | Fig. No. 2,   Do. |
| Do.   Do., Altered at the Summit, in order to obtain the whole supply of the District, | 32 | 230 | 178 | 43 or 60 ft. | 5.60 | 19 | 4,400, including 260 acres of Lakes. | Fig. No. 3 & 4, Do. |
| The Ballinamuck Line, { Canal, 23½ ; River & Lake, 14 } | 37½ | 191 | 103 | 32  6 | 4.00† | 11 | Not ascertained, but believed to be insufficient. | Fig. No. 5,   Do. |

March 11th, 1839.

W. T. MULVANY.

* 5.75 is the rate of Lockage on the Canal portion of this line.
† 4.00 is the rate of Lockage on the Canal portion of this line.

Fig. 2. Three possible routes, surveyed by W. T. Mulvany, 1839

courses or other expensive works'. The line was very similar to that proposed by Chapman 45 years earlier, leaving the Shannon at Leitrim village, 'at the harbour proposed to be formed by the Shannon Commissioners, as the northern terminus of the Inland Steam Navigation of the Shannon', and running along the valley of the Leitrim River to Letterfine, 'where the average depth of cutting to obtain the required supply would be but 13 feet 6 inches, for a length of 2,400 yards'. From this summit the canal would be laid out 'under all the advantageous circumstances of gradually falling ground, through the valley of Ballinamore, to join the River Erne, a little above the town of Belturbet', and the way to the Ulster Canal would then be via the proposed lock in Belturbet.

Mulvany had a general knowledge of the country through which the line would run but, as he had not 'perambulated it in detail', he was not very specific about the route east of Ballinamore and he spelt out two possibilities. The line could be brought as a canal to Killeshandra whence the river would be followed to Belturbet, or the length of river navigation could be reduced to one mile by 'the construction of 4 additional miles of Canal in the direct line'. In either case he felt that the line would be the most suitable from both commercial and engineering points of view.

It had been part of Mulvany's brief to report on the 'Traffic and the Amount of Commercial Benefit' likely to arise if a canal were built and the latter part of his report was devoted to this aspect. At that time Newry and Belfast were the chief trading ports for the countryside between the Erne and Letterfine (itself only 5 miles from the Shannon), and to 'Ballinamore, within 14 miles of the Shannon, even the heavy article of timber is frequently brought by land carriage from Newry and Belfast'. Even towns like Mohill and Boyle which would have much trade with Dublin would still send much of their livestock and agricultural produce to the north along the canal. A list of specific traffics which Mulvany thought would materialise read quite impressively. It included coal 'from the Arigna and

other Collieries in the neighbourhood of Lough Allen', iron
'from Arigna to the foundries at Belfast and the North of
Ireland', livestock and so on. The report even noted that slates
and marble from Killaloe 'may be expected to be sent through
this canal to the North', and Mulvany, while not venturing a
precise estimate of the traffic, was of the firm opinion that the
canal would be of a 'remunerative nature'.

Although the relative haste with which the investigation
was made precluded Mulvany from making any sort of detailed
survey of the country through which the Ballinamore line
would run, he did not overlook the all-important question of
cost. Taking as the basis for his calculations 'the full cost, per
mile, of the Ulster Canal, inclusive of very heavy Parliamentary
expenses'—which he hoped would 'in future be avoided in
works of Public utility'—Mulvany set out the probable cost.[5]

| | |
|---|---:|
| 28½ miles of canal, including Locks, Bridges &c., at £5,000 per mile ................. | £142,500 |
| Lock, regulating Weir, and other works at Belturbet, say........................... | £10,000 |
| Shoal between Belturbet and terminus of Ulster Canal, say ...................... | £ 500 |
| Total for Canal from Leitrim to Belturbet, and thence to Ulster Canal .................. | £153,000 |
| Probable cost of removing Shoals, altering Bridges, and improving navigation for steam vessels from Belturbet by the River Erne and Lough Oughter to Killeshandra | £ 14,000 |
| | £167,000 |

Mulvany concluded his report with the remark that were the
proposed Shannon works to be carried out, the advantages of
the junction canal would be very considerable and 'perhaps
render it deserving of a proportionate share of public support
and control'. In the event of the Shannon works not being
undertaken he thought the canal would carry the whole trade
of the region it served and that this would 'probably . . . render

it a fit speculation for private enterprise'. If the latter were the case he thought most of the traffic would go on through the Ulster Canal and that then the locks on the junction canal needed only to be built to the smaller dimensions of the former waterway. But he added a rider:

> But as the projects for the improvement of the Upper Shannon are now under the consideration of the Legislature, and it is to be presumed will soon be carried into effect, and as the additional expenditure which would be incurred in adopting the larger scale of the Royal and Grand Canals would not be considerable, and would arise chiefly from a small increase in the size of the locks, it seems desirable that the grand object of making this a Junction Canal common to all the principal navigations of Ireland, should not, on account of this additional expenditure, be lost to the public.[6]

Persuasive as the tone of Mulvany's report was, it evidently met with a lack of interest as no action was taken on it and the idea was shelved. Possibly the Treasury remained unconvinced of the value which might be returned on the expenditure of a sum nearly a third of that budgeted for the works along the whole Shannon, altogether a more important waterway. But the project was to come very much to the fore again within a very few years, the stimulus coming from the passing of the first of a very important series of Acts in 1842.

The first navigation Act of 1715 included the important topic of land drainage in its scope, and interest was to focus repeatedly on the drainage question, appropriately for a country with vast expanses of boggy land. Various moves were made with a view to encouraging the improvement of land by drainage, chief among them being the appointment of Commissioners of Bog Improvement, who held office from September 1807 until December 1813. Their deliberations and surveys cost £37,221 and their findings were enshrined in voluminous reports but, unhappily, no actual works of drainage were carried out.[7] The position was more or less unchanged up to the 1840s, but in 1842 a highly significant event

was the passing of the Act 5 & 6 Vic, c 89—the basic Act of
the code of Irish arterial drainage law.

Enacted on 5 August 1842, this Act of 162 sections stimulated a vast programme of arterial drainage works throughout
Ireland undertaken by the BOW, whose members were appointed the commissioners for its execution. Its relevance in
the context of waterways is expressed in its title—'An Act to
promote the Drainage of Lands, and Improvement of Navigation and Water Power in connexion with such Drainage, in
*Ireland*'. Although subsequent legislation modified some of the
provisions of this first Act, many of its sections formed the
base on which a very limited number of navigations, including
the Ballinamore Canal, were made.

The Act specified the procedures which were to be followed
by persons interested in drainage or navigation projects. Any-
body having an interest in flooded land, or land capable of
being drained, or in the making navigable or the improvement
of any river could request the BOW by memorial to carry out
the desired improvements. Grand Juries could also make such
memorials and all memorialists were required to lodge a sum of
money to meet the expenses of the preliminary inspection, inquiry and report by the BOW. This was the 'first deposit' and
a second was required to be paid if the preliminary assessment
of the project was favourable, being expended on 'further
Surveys, Schedules, Maps, Plans, Drawings, Sections and
Estimate'.

On receipt of the first deposit the BOW directed 'some
Engineer or other competent Person' to survey the area of
interest and to investigate the proposals for drainage, and possibly navigation as well, taking note of the probable benefits to
be derived from any work carried out. Mills were also to be
considered both from the point of view of acquiring and improving them. The inspector would report to the BOW as to
the probable expense of the proposed works and if his report
met with approval it was printed and made available to the
public on sale and for inspection for a specified time.

The next stage in the proceedings was the collection of the second deposits from the interested parties, after which a much more detailed survey would be carried out and plans, sections and estimates drawn up. Schedules would be prepared showing the lands which would be improved by the drainage and the cost of the works involved, and also—most important—'the Proportions in which such Lands shall contribute towards the payment of the Costs'. The estimated navigation costs would be shown separately and the 'District likely to be benefited by such Improvement' and the 'Baronies, Half-Baronies or Townlands' which would have to bear the cost would also be specified.

Copies of the 'Schedules, Maps, Plans, Sections and Estimate' would then be deposited for 6 weeks' public inspection, a notice being issued to this effect. Any objections could then be lodged and the BOW was empowered to hold public meetings at which the proposals would be discussed and objections considered. Once agreed modifications had been made to the plans the BOW would receive the 'Assents in Writing of the Proprietors of the Lands' detailed in the schedules, the consent of the owners of at least two-thirds of the land to be improved being necessary before the works could be commenced.

In the case of the proposed making or improvement of a navigation the grand juries of the district 'likely to be benefited' were empowered to approve the works and to undertake to pay their cost. No work was to start until such a declaration had been received from the county authorities and assents received from proprietors of two-thirds of the land adjacent to the proposed navigation. In addition the payment of at least two-thirds of the estimated cost had to be guaranteed by grand jury presentment before work could begin. Where a proprietor's land was occupied by tenants it was necessary to have an assent from the tenant as well.

Once the required assents had been received from the proprietors the BOW made a formal declaration of the extent of the lands to be improved, their present and increased value after drainage, the charge to be levied on them and their proprietors. This declaration was a vitally important document and it also specified the proposed navigation improvements, setting out the district which would benefit from the work and which would pay for it, and also giving the details of any mills which would be interfered with by the BOW, which had quite wide powers in this respect. The declaration was then lodged for inspection by the public and, if there were no appeals against the BOW proposals, the board then published a 'final notice' stating that all the requirements of the Act had been fully complied with. This was the last stage in what were quite complicated preliminary proceedings, and the publication of the final notice was conclusive. Those who had paid their deposits possibly a long time previously now received their money back (which they would not have done had the BOW vetoed the scheme) and work could then begin.

The many sections of the Act covered a variety of topics from the employment of workmen to the charging of navigation tolls, but even so an amending Act had to be passed three years later, in July 1845.[8] Its provisions covered financial matters principally, though it tightened up the general procedure a little. For example, a memorandum of the BOW declaration was to be made and registered, and no appeals would be heard unless notice in writing was given within 21 days of the making of the declaration. Those declarations previously made were required to be registered. Attention was also given to the proprietors' assents and a specified form was ordered to be used in all cases.

A further amending Act was passed in March 1846 to modify the procedure, largely as a result of experience gained from some three years' operation of the 1842 provisions.[9] For example, there had been delays and difficulties in obtaining assents 'by reason of the Absence of many Proprietors' and it was now permissible to proceed once the assents of the owners of half the lands to be improved had been received. The preliminary survey procedure was shortened and, under section 17, the BOW was permitted to 'affix a Name to each District' by which the district would thereafter be 'known, called, and described'. The Act also touched on navigation matters, the principal feature being that Parliament could grant 'a Moiety or more of the Expence' of making the navigation.

This Act of 1846 contained other important provisions, which were to have a complicating effect on the Ballinamore project. These were appended to the earlier sections, which largely modified the earlier Acts. That they were included in the Act reflected some concern over the social situation in Ireland at the time. The potato crop was then the basic food of the Irish peasantry and it had begun to fail from blight in autumn 1845. Six months later starvation was already quite common and panic was setting in—the Great Famine had begun. Some relief measures were undertaken; committees were set up and some quite worthless relief works were commissioned.

Rather more valuable, however, was the alteration to the drainage procedure authorised by the 1846 Act, 9 Vic, c 4. Under section 45 were made 'Provisions of a more summary Nature . . . whereby remunerative Employment [might] be afforded to the labouring Classes'. Known as the 'Provisions for summary Proceedings', they allowed for an even shorter preliminary procedure to be followed for schemes for which assents were received by 1 August 1847, in the case of drainage works only. The time scale was shortened and the preliminary investigation could be carried out 'in a summary way'. A final notice could be issued as soon as assents had been received and works could then begin. Their scope was limited, however, and the expenditure was required to be limited to an average of £3 per acre of land improved. However, the works could afterwards be carried on under the 'ordinary Proceedings' of the 1842 Act when further assents were forthcoming.

Yet another amending Act was passed in July 1847 and it too reflected the critical state of the Irish nation, in that it con-

Page 33   Locks: (*above*) Castlefore, looking west; (*below*) the fine Lock No 11 at Kilclare

*Page 34* Peaceful waters: (*above*) west of Ballyduff, showing the old navigation channel on the right; (*below*) the basin at Ballinamore. The railway ran across the blind arches on the right

tinued for a further year the operation of the summary proceedings provisions, introducing at the same time a further
short cut.[10] Now the assents of the proprietors alone would
suffice for drainage works irrespective of whether or not the
occupiers of the lands agreed to the proposals. Great delay had
been experienced with tenants' assents and the new move was
bound to make the procedure less cumbersome. The short Act
also fixed very definitely the responsibilities of the grand juries
of a navigation district to pay the rest of the cost outstanding
after a free grant had been made. The charges necessary were
to be levied directly off the area without the usual grand jury
presentments being made.

These four Acts formed the basic code of drainage-cum-
navigation law and, although a further series of Acts was to be
passed nearly a decade later, it was according to their provisions
that the BOW energetically began a programme of drainage
schemes throughout the country. One of the major projects
was the Ballinamore & Ballyconnell, and the various steps in
its development illustrate perfectly the working of the Acts.

CHAPTER 3

# The Birth of the Project
# (1844–1852)

The intermixture of the navigation and drainage
works is perplexing.

*BOW Chairman, 1854*

THE inception of the Ballinamore and Ballyconnell drainage
and navigation project was a lengthy and highly complicated
process. Not only were different interests bound together, but
the drainage works were begun under the summary proceedings of 9 Vic, c 4 and later continued in conjunction with the
navigation scheme under the ordinary proceedings of 5 & 6
Vic, c 89. In all, over 3½ years elapsed from the first tentative
inquiries to the final 'all-clear' for the joint project. This was,
however, not surprising as the scheme was but one—admittedly a major one—of a total of over 120 which the BOW
undertook as a result of the 1842 Act.

It was the passing of this Act which stimulated the landowners of Leitrim and Cavan to make a request for a drainage
scheme, but probably the greatest impetus for a navigation
project came from another event of 1842—the completion of
the 46-mile Ulster Canal from Charlemont on the River Black-
water to Wattle Bridge on the Erne. This waterway, despite its
narrow locks, was made 'as an important section of a great
composite waterway which was to be formed across Ireland',[1]
and now that it was completed the Ulster Canal Company was
very anxious to extend westwards to the Shannon. Conse-

quently it was not long before the company made some practical moves to achieve its goal.

The first moves, however, were for a drainage scheme. On 1 March 1844 the BOW received from Francis Latouche a memorial from the landed proprietors seeking a scheme to improve some 2,400 acres in the region between Ballinamore and Ballyheady Bridge.[2] The BOW on 20 March requested those concerned to lodge £60 as the first deposit for the preliminary investigation, it being reckoned that a further £190 would suffice as the second deposit for the more detailed surveys. Within a month the deposits were being paid in by the landowners and the investigation was extended suitably when a second memorial was received praying that the drainage might be extended from Ballyheady to Ballyconnell.

No mention had yet been made of navigation, but the question was shortly considered and the BOW on 8 June applied to the Shannon Commissioners for the use of Mulvany's plans and report of 1839. Meanwhile an engineer, John McMahon, was carrying out the preliminary survey and the feasibility of the project was soon evident, for on 5 August Charles Brassington was commissioned to make the valuation and detailed survey of the extended district 'from the site of the old lock at Corquill' [Caroul] to Ballinamore. He was instructed to furnish full information 'as to the extent and nature of the flooded lands, the duration of the floods, and the benefit to be derived from the proposed works',[3] and to aid in the collection of data the BOW sent a rain gauge to Ballinamore on 27 August.

Perhaps because people were getting to hear of this activity further interest was expressed in the project and about the beginning of September 1844 a request was made for the further extension of the district. Through Dr Robert Collins a memorial came from 'the proprietors of land adjoining the rivers and lakes near Keshcarrigan and Ballinamore, in the county of Leitrim, for the drainage of lands in that locality as a continuation of the Ballinamore Drainage'.[4] The BOW agreed that 'the whole of the lands from Letterfine to Ballyconnell should form

one district' and sought a further £150 in deposits. A further
memorial was to follow shortly from the Ulster Canal Company.

The UCC had written to the BOW on 3 August asking for a
statement of the expense needed for surveys and seeking an
opinion as to the best point where a canal might join the Woodford River, and in its reply the latter pointed out that no works
were in progress but that deposits had been lodged for the
surveys and valuations of the lands east of Ballinamore. As yet
there had been no formal application for drainage work west
of Ballinamore but the BOW knew one would soon be made.
It was estimated that £350 would meet the cost of the preliminary investigation for a navigation scheme and the 'proper
mode of proceeding' was pointed out.[5]

The UCC responded fairly quickly and on 9 October made a
formal memorial to the BOW. Within a week a contribution of
£100 was made and later the whole £350 was deposited. By the
time of the UCC inquiry the BOW was of the opinion that the
navigation scheme was a good one and, in a letter of 12 August
to Lord Eliot of the Irish Office, it had set out the outline proposals, stating their usefulness, and proffering the opinion that
the measure should be carried out 'under the provisions of the
Drainage Act, in which every necessary power is contained,
and by which, whoever provides the funds, the navigation
would remain in the hands of the Commissioners', the alloca-
tion of the tolls being provided for. The BOW thought that it
would be 'excellent policy' for the Government to grant aid to
the project.[6]

Once the UCC memorial and deposit had been received the
way was clear for the BOW to have the necessary surveys made
of the entire district and on 2 November 1844 John McMahon,
then busy in the region east of Ballinamore, was told 'to take
the necessary steps to have the inquiry extended accordingly
from Lough Erne to the Shannon at Leitrim'. McMahon was
told that it seemed likely that the Woodford River could be
followed for all but four or five miles of the route and he was
directed to pay special attention to land drainage in the section

west of Lough Scur, where a canal would be needed, and also
to the control of the mountain rivers from the viewpoints of
flood control and of providing a water supply for the navigation and the mills along its course. His brief also stated

> It is advisable to investigate the practicability of shortening and
> improving the line of navigation by an artificial canal from St
> John's Lough by the village of Eddentinny to the Woodford
> River at or near Waterdale [*recto* Lawderdale].[7]

In other words, he was to consider avoiding the loop around
by Ballinamore town—seemingly an ill-advised suggestion
from the commercial point of view. McMahon was informed
that the navigation 'should be suited to small class steamers
worked either by paddles placed at the stern or the screw pro-
pellor' and he was warned to be economical as those interested
in the 'navigation part of this inquiry' had been told that £350
would meet all preliminary expenses. To complete his task he
was required to afford information on the utility of the navigation as a link waterway and to give 'fullest information' on
local traffic prospects.

Thus at the end of 1844 a detailed land valuation programme
was being carried on by Brassington, while the engineering
inquiry was in the hands of McMahon assisted by a team including William Forsyth, William Frazer, Charles Gerrard and
James Peacock. Their services were charged to the navigation
account—section 104 of the 1842 Act had laid down that navigation and drainage accounts were to be kept separately—while
the remuneration of Charles Ottley, the engineer engaged on
the drainage survey, came from the drainage account.
McMahon's connection with the district was to cease in 1848
but Forsyth would bear a greater or lesser degree of responsibility for almost all the lengthy period of construction.

By May 1845 McMahon's report was ready and it was soon
followed by one from Brassington, who received a fee of 9d (4p)
for each of the 6,253 acres which he estimated would be relieved by the proposed works. Of this area 4,733 acres suffered
from floods while the rest remained in a wet and swampy state.

The benefit to the land was estimated at £1,897 or an average of just over 6s (30p) an acre. The other report spelt out the probable cost of achieving this relief from flooding and also of effecting a junction navigation between the Shannon and the Erne. McMahon put the cost of the drainage works at £23,267 and that for the navigation at £103,000, but he thought that if the works were executed jointly the aggregate cost would fall to £110,301. All sums were exclusive of interest payable on money borrowed for the works.[8]

The BOW approved of the report and its proposals and on 27 June wrote to Francis Latouche, the UCC and the Grand Juries of Cavan, Leitrim and Fermanagh stating that the works would be executed jointly for drainage and navigation. On the following day the abstract of the valuation was circulated to all interested parties and a letter went to Roscommon Grand Jury noting that there was 'reason to hope that the benefits to be derived from the works, in the event of their being executed, may extend to that county'.[9] This was an interesting move and was possibly made as a 'softening-up' of the grand jury of a county through which the navigation would at no point pass and which would derive absolutely no benefit from the drainage measures. However, if the navigation was the success expected, then it would undoubtedly bring some benefit to the northern part of the county, possibly even leading to a revival of the fortunes of the Arigna coal and iron district.

The occurrence of the phrase 'in the event of their being executed' in the letter indicated that the approval of the commissioners was not sufficient to initiate the works, a similar doubt being expressed in July in a reply to a memorial from the labourers in the vicinity of Ballinamore inquiring when the works would commence. It was stated then that no start would be made in 1845 nor, indeed, was it certain that they would be undertaken. Presumably the reasons underlying these doubts were financial, but whatever their nature they did not immediately interrupt the progress of the formal proceedings. By a notice dated 7 August 1845 the BOW announced that the preliminary report had been deposited with the Clerks of the Peace and Secretaries of the Grand Juries of Cavan, Leitrim and Fermanagh, and that copies were available for public inspection and on sale at 6d (2½p) at Enniskillen, Belturbet, Carrick-on-Shannon, Swanlinbar, Ballinamore and Ballyconnell. After this, however, there was an interruption or, as it was put 14 years later by two commissioners, 'some delay . . . appears to have taken place in the subsequent proceedings'.

The matter was raised again early in 1846 when a memorial was received from some of the landowners requesting that the district be brought under the summary proceedings of 9 Vic, c 4 as a relief measure. As was related later:

---

## DRAINAGF.
### Under the Act 5th and 6th Vic., Ch. 89.

### DISTRICT OF
### BALLINAMORÉ & BALLYCONNELL,
#### COUNTIES LEITRIM, CAVAN, and FERMANAGH.

**N**OTICE is hereby given, that COPIES of the PRELIMINARY REPORT on the proposed Drainage of the FLOODED LANDS in the District of Ballinamore and Ballyconnell, in the counties of Leitrim, Cavan, and Fermanagh, and on the Line of the Junction Navigation for connecting Lough Erne and the River Shannon, required to be made under the provisions of the Act 5th and 6th Victoria, c. 89, HAVE BEEN DEPOSITED with the Clerks of the Peace, and Secretaries of the Grand Juries of the Counties Leitrim, Cavan, and Fermanagh, respectively. and copies of said Report have also been deposited with Mrs Willes, White Hart Hotel, Enniskillen ; Mr E. Fitzpatrick, Hotel, Belturbet ; Mr H Church, Hotel, Carrick on-Shannon : Mr Thos. Nugent, Hotel, Swanlinbar ; Mr D. Thompson, Hotel, Ballinamore ; and Mr Patrick Kane, Hotel, Ballyconnell, to remain open for public inspection for six successive weeks, as by said Act required, and copies of said Report may be obtained on application at any of the above-mentioned hotels, or at the Office of Public Works, Custom House, Dublin. for the sum of Sixpence each.
By Order of the Commissioners.
            **HENRY R. PAINE, Secretary.**
Dated at the Office of Public Works,
    Custom House, Dublin, this
        7th day of August 1845.

FIG 3. Notice of deposit of Preliminary Report, 1845

In compliance with this request Mr McMahon was accordingly instructed to prepare without delay a short report based on his previous one, which having been done without loss of time the necessary steps were taken in printing, lodging and circulating it, for collecting the assents of the proprietors, the area of improveable land being the same as set forth in Mr Brassington's schedule, and the estimated cost of the works the lesser amount calculated on the assumption of their being carried out in conjunction with the navigation, or £19,000, it being understood as specially requested by the memorialists that the adopting of this course should in no way interfere with the accomplishment of the latter measure which was characterised by them as being of 'vital importance to the country at large'.[10]

Certainly no time was lost. On 7 May 1846 notice was given of the deposit of the reports for inspection and just seven weeks later sufficient assents had been collected to allow the final notice to be issued. The notice was the 22nd to be issued and was dated 26 June 1846. Under it the way was clear for the drainage to be commenced and carried on to the limited extent permitted by the provisions for summary proceedings. Work commenced on 30 June in charge of William Forsyth. Some indication of its nature is given by a few of the orders for supplies placed soon afterwards:

| | | | |
|---|---|---|---|
| 7 July | Richard A. Gray | 200 wheelbarrows | £110 |
| 25 August | } W. H. Enery | Wheelbarrows, | |
| 26 September | | shovels etc. | £210 |
| 15 September | Stewart Leckey | Spades | £15 |

This commencement under the summary proceedings was something of a stop-gap and the BOW now turned its attention to the ordinary proceedings which had to be followed in order to get the navigation measure off the ground. One of the most important questions was that of financing the work and here the Treasury had helped. By a 'minute of 20 March 1846 [it] approved of granting a moiety of the cost peculiar to navigation'.[11] The grant was made in response to a request from the Irish administration and the Cavan Grand Jury. The amount was subsequently fixed at £46,250, 'the moiety without interest of the estimated cost'. An apportionment was then made of 'the other moiety or £49,625' over those areas of Cavan, Leitrim, Fermanagh and Roscommon which were deemed to be the beneficiaries of the navigation, and a copy of the apportionment document was lodged for inspection.

This latter amount would be levied on completion of the works and it would thus be necessary to borrow money to carry on during the period of construction. The Acts provided that loans could be obtained from individuals (in return for which they would receive debentures), but it was also possible to obtain Government loans. As it turned out this was a necessary alternative, for a mere £7,500 was raised from individuals, William Boothe who provided £2,500 and a Dr Johnson who lent the rest, in July 1846.[12] The remaining vast sums needed for the construction came from Government funds. Pressed though the BOW may have been for money, it followed the rules strictly and at the same time repaid the £265 which had been subscribed for the preliminary drainage expenses and which had to be refunded once the scheme was approved.

On 4 August 1846 the BOW gave notice of the deposit of the reports, plans and estimates for the drainage-cum-navigation measure under the ordinary proceedings and of its intention to hold a meeting at the Courthouse, Ballinamore on 8 September to consider the matter. It was at this meeting that applications for extensions to the district, in its drainage aspect, were made and, however valuable they may have been, they meant that much further work had to be done on the plans. Both Brassington and McMahon had to enter the picture again, the former to value the additional lands and the latter to consider the engineering aspects and to furnish a revised estimate of the costs. At the end of November McMahon was being urged to make the revised estimate, the matter being 'very pressing', but he was not in a position to make his report for some months yet. Forsyth came up with a revised estimate on 22 December. His figure of £132,659 turned out to be very close to the mark, for when McMahon submitted his revised

report and estimate on 4 March 1847 his final figure was
£131,858, made up as follows:

Drainage works—chargeable to proprietors    £27,110
Drainage—works of masonry in connexion
 therewith, chargeable to counties    £ 4,582
Navigation works—chargeable to Government
 grant and to four counties    £100,166

£131,858[13]

The difference of £21,557 between the original and revised
estimates for the joint measure was attributable to the additional drainage to be carried out, extra charges for labour,
interest charges on borrowed money and general increases in
the scale of the proposed works; for example, the enlargement
of the sectional area of the waterway.

Such substantial revisions of the plans and estimates meant
that the whole tedious business of sending the report to the
interested parties and of collecting renewed assents had to be
repeated. Throughout the first half of 1847 assents were being
sought, considered and granted but the whole business was
slow—slow enough, in fact, to halt the drainage work then in
progress under the summary proceedings. On 7 August
Forsyth was told

A sum of £3 per acre has been expended in the Ballinamore &
Ballyconnell District and as the assents under the ordinary
proceedings are not yet perfect the Board direct that you will
stop all works in this District until further orders.[14]

However, by 30 September all the assents had been received
and the formal declaration had been signed, notice of its deposit
for inspection being given on 9 October. While the last assents
were coming in Forsyth was told to furnish information on all
the mills between the Shannon and the Erne which would be
interfered with during the works.

Once the declaration had been signed and not objected to the
way was clear for the issue of the final notice. Forsyth mean-

time was given careful instructions on what he was to do regarding the work:

> I am directed by the Board to instruct you to resume and proceed with the works for drainage, not commencing those for navigation until after the issue of the second Final Notice.[15]

There was not too long more to wait. On 16 November the BOW solicitor was instructed to issue the final notice, and this he did 3 days later, the final 'all-clear' being given on 19 November 1847. The one remaining preliminary task was to refund the UCC deposit of £350—a sum which the company

## BOARD OF PUBLIC WORKS.
## DRAINAGE and NAVIGATION.
Under the Acts 5th & 6th Vict, chap 89—8th & 9th Vic, chap 69—9th Vic, chap 4—and 10th & 11th Vic, chap 79.

# DISTRICT of BALLINAMORE and BALLYCONNELL,
### in the COUNTIES of CAVAN, FERMANAGH, LEITRIM, and ROSCOMMON.

## FINAL NOTICE
### Of Compliance
with the requisites of the above mentioned Acts.

We, the Commissioners of Public Works in Ireland, acting in execution of the above mentioned Acts, do hereby notify and declare, that the several Preliminary Measures and Proceedings by the Act of the 5th and 6th Vict, chap 89, entitled "An Act to promote the Drainage of Lands, and Improvement of Navigation and Water Power in connexion with such Drainage in Ireland," and the several Acts amending the same, directed to be taken and observed, previously to the commencement of the proposed Works in the District of Ballinamore and Ballyconnell, in the counties of Cavan, Fermanagh, Leitrim, and Roscommon. HAVE BEEN CONCLUDED. And we do hereby GIVE THIS FINAL NOTICE, that all the requisitions of the said Acts with respect to the lands within the said District proposed to be Drained and Improved, and also with respect to the making and improving of Navigation within said District HAVE BEEN COMPLIED WITH.

HARRY D. JONES ⎫ Two of the Commissioners of
THOS A. LARCOM ⎭ Public Works in Ireland.
Dated at the Office of Public Works,
Custom House, Dublin,
this 19th day of November 1847,

FIG 4. The second 'Final Notice', as published in the *General Advertiser*, 1847

was extraordinarily anxious to recover—and this was done on 31 January 1848.

The first work in the district had begun on 30 June 1846 and for a period of well over a year effort was concentrated on the drainage measure under the summary proceedings, the work affording 'a large amount of relief by reproductive employment'. Many hundreds of labourers were employed. Their equipment was primitive—the barrows, picks and shovels bought in 1846—and it was supplemented in December 1847 by further quantities of similar tools provided from the famine relief stores at Belturbet, Cavan, Sligo, Enniskillen and Swanlinbar. The work was within an ace of being suspended in November 1847 after an 'attack on the collector of county cess in the parish of Fenagh' but after the matter had been considered by the Lord Lieutenant the threatened suspension was not carried out. However, an interruption was soon to occur, the cause being a want of funds which Forsyth said 'disconcerted our plans'. Early in 1848 there was no money for the drainage work, but the navigation works which had been started by then were allowed to continue 'to as great extent as is consistent with efficiency and economy'. The unsatisfactory position was explained to Forsyth a little later:

> In the navigation works you are not limited by any given sum per month—in the purely drainage works you are limited by the sum now available for those works.[16]

The net result was a 'stop-go' policy under which men were hired and suddenly released. It was unfortunate that some of the fallow periods came at a time when distress prevailed throughout the country, and when the parish priest of Carrick-on-Shannon wrote requesting that the poor be employed on the drainage works the BOW was unable to meet his request. Neither could it respond favourably to the memorial of labourers who had been employed on the drainage works but who had been discharged. It was not until well into 1849 that the drainage works were resumed in the district, which was designated a distressed area by the Government.

However, despite the interruptions, the works brought quite a degree of relief to the farmers of the region. By the end of 1848 the lands east of Caroul were relieved of summer and autumn floods although they were 'still under the influence of Lough Erne in winter'.[17] Between Caroul and Ballyconnell there was complete relief and varying degrees of improvement were reported the whole way westwards to Castlefore. This was good progress, especially as there had been an abnormal rainfall early in 1848 and even in summer 'at intervals sudden high and destructive floods impeded the works most injuriously'. Rain was also exceptionally heavy in the autumn of the following year, again causing interruptions to the works.

By then T. J. Mulvany was in charge, having taken over from Forsyth. In December 1849 he was instructed that 'the works at the summit level should be pushed forward with as much vigour as possible, both with a view to employment and to an early completion of the works'. Three months later he was warned that 'not a day of this season is to be lost . . . the works in the mountain streams are to be vigorously carried on'. Mulvany pressed on as instructed and at the end of 1850 was able to report considerable progress. He had met with one unexpected difficulty, however, a scarcity of labour. There was less local demand for work and the maximum number of men at work on any one day was 2,650, a third less than in 1849. There was not such a drop in the daily average numbers of workers, but further declines were to come in subsequent years. A factor of no little importance was the state of the weather, especially in summer. If it was fine the men preferred to stay on their farms, attending to their harvest.

But the rise and fall in the number of labourers gave quite a good indication of the progress being made on the works, especially as far as the excavation of the river and canal channels was concerned. By 1848 much work had been done in the Ballyconnell/Caroul reach and the outfalls of Coologe and St John's Loughs had been cleared. At the end of 1849 the main channel was in a very forward state, the stretch from Ballyconnell to the Erne being nearly finished. In the reaches from Garadice to St John's Lough and from Drumany to Lough Scur, as well as on almost the whole length of the new navigation cut from Lough Scur to Leitrim, progress was good and it was anticipated that all the earthwork would be finished early next season.

Mulvany also expressed satisfaction with the progress at the most difficult spot—the heavy rock cutting on the summit level at Letterfine, west of Lough Scur. To aid in operations here a railway was proposed and in March 1850 it was ordered that 'rails should be laid down for the Letterfine Rock cut and the spoil run out to Lough Scur, as moles into a deep-water harbour, and thus obviate the necessity of uselessly occupying the land'.[18] Some 50 tons of rails, 883 in all, were dispatched to Mulvany in July on 'Pilsworth's boat' and by the end of the year a horse tramway was in operation. Work had also continued on the main channel on filling in the gaps along the route, at Ballyheady, the Aghoo/Ballinamore reach, and near Castlefore. In addition, the 'course of the river between Lough Marrave and Lough Scur, which was exceedingly swampy, [was] carefully drained and consolidated preparatory to the excavation of the navigable channel'.

Work continued throughout 1851 and 1852 at places where there were shoals—Coologe, Skelan, Woodford and Ballyconnell—and by the end of the latter year the Letterfine cut was complete, bringing to a virtual conclusion the work on the artificial cut from Lough Scur to the Shannon. By this time excavation had given way to dredging, along the main channel. As early as 1849 a hand dredger had been brought to the district and used at Aghalane and a 'spoon and bag' dredger was also fitted up. In 1850 larger dredgers were transferred to the district, on paper at any rate, a sum of £713 being charged for the transfer of 'B' and 'E' dredgers formerly used on the Shannon works. In fact the former seems not to have been used on the canal, while the latter was stripped of its engine and machinery before being returned to its owner. It was decided to use the salvaged equipment in a dredger to be built specially for the district.[19]

The Shannon works were by this time virtually complete and the workshops at Rooskey were no longer needed. The BOW bought the tools and equipment and made an agreement with 'Mr Reilly of Liverpool, the proprietor of a large yard and garden together with a small dwelling house' at Belturbet by which it set up offices and workshops there for the Ballinamore & Ballyconnell and other adjacent districts. The details had been settled by May 1850 and shortly afterwards the workshops were in action, turning out much iron and timber work. It was decided to build the dredger at Belturbet and John Lynch was chosen to supervise the work, which went on for nearly two years. In 1852 it was reported that 'a large steam dredger', 80ft long by 15ft 6in beam, made of timber, along with 'two scows or tenders', 48ft by 15ft, had been built and 'launched and fitted with steam engine, boiler and other machinery'. It was soon to prove very useful in continuing the dredging, which had gone on principally in the Coologe–Ballyconnell–Aghalane region, and which would be continued for a long time to come.

While the greater effort had initially been concentrated necessarily on the excavation and preparation of the main navigation channel, work was in progress concurrently on the other engineering features of the navigation. One of the first questions to be dealt with was that of bridges, which was sub-divided under three headings. Firstly, quite a number of completely new road bridges had to be built over the new navigation cuts and on the new courses of the feeder rivers. Secondly, there were the smaller but quite numerous accommodation bridges which had to be provided across the main channel and over lateral drainage channels at places where lands had been severed or where old fords had been swept away. Finally, there were the bridges over the river courses involved in the navigation, which had existed long before the commencement of the works but which required alteration or reconstruction.

Under section 60 of the 1842 Act any bridge over a river,

carrying a public or county road, which in the opinion of the BOW was 'insufficient for the free Discharge' of flood water could be 'reconstructed in such Manner as . . . shall seem sufficient'. The commissioners had to determine 'by a Declaration in Writing under their Hands and Seals' the apportionment of the expense of the reconstruction on the region—counties, baronies or half-baronies—served by the bridge. The declaration was published and once any objections had been dealt with the Grand Juries of the counties concerned were obliged to present their respective portions of the cost of the work and they were thenceforth responsible for maintenance.

These were the so-called 'county works', and the bridges in the district in this category included those at Aghalane, Ballyconnell, Ballyheady and that over the river channel at Ballinamore; others were over the various drainage arteries. The 'county works' were among the first to be carried out, although the first declarations were not made until 1852. In the first six years of the works some 20 bridges were built or completely rebuilt. Most were fine masonry structures, though some of the smaller accommodation bridges were either of timber or wrought iron executed at the Belturbet workshops set up in 1850.

Lock construction began in 1848 along the river section of the navigation and at each of the eight locations a weir had also to be built to maintain a water depth adequate for boats. Provision had also to be made for large sluices beside the weirs to permit the rapid discharge of flood waters. Later on a decision was made to provide a fish pass alongside each weir. By the end of 1850 three of the river locks had been almost completed while materials had been prepared for building three more. By then, too, the masonry of half of the remaining eight locks, on the still-water section west of Lough Scur, had been completed and progress was very advanced on the rest. The average estimated cost of the locks was £1,500, of which £1,300 was for masonry. The building of the lock gates began late in 1850, much of the work being done at Belturbet, but the locks were

Page 51 Construction detail: (*above*) dilapidated masonry in the 'island' between the lock and the weir at Aghoo; (*right*) iron sluice gear at Ballyduff; (*below*) the fish pass at Ballyconnell

Page 52 Bridges—1: (*above*) the very fine skew bridge at Kilclare; (*below*) Aghalane Bridge, with the Republic of Ireland frontier station in the background

not nearly ready for use by the end of 1852; indeed, Skelan lock had not even been started. Likewise, several years were to elapse before the weirs were completed.

One task which was finished early on, however, was the construction of three wharves along the canal. By late 1850 the wharves at Ballyconnell, Ballinamore and Leitrim had been completed, and another work very well advanced was the diversion of 'the course of the mountain streams into the lakes which lie along the line of the navigation'. The need for the latter was later explained:

> It was also considered necessary in order to keep the canal free from interruption as far as practicable after completion that the courses of the Yellow and Aghacashlaun Rivers should be diverted by new lines of discharge into St John's Lake and Lough Scur respectively, at the point where they approach these lakes thereby providing for the throwing down and depositing of the large quantities of sand and gravel with which they are charged in time of floods at places where neither the navigation nor the drainage would be injuriously affected.[20]

In fact, two rivers were diverted into Lough Scur—the Driney (or Kiltubrid) River which was channelled through a new rock cut to the western side of the lake, and the Aghacashlaun River which formerly flowed down to Castlefore and thence east-wards to St John's Lough at Muckros; the latter river was now diverted westwards into Lough Scur. Both these diversions were essentially complete by the end of 1851 and the same was true of the Yellow River which, instead of flowing south-eastwards to Creevy now swung to the south-west through Kiltybarden to the northernmost tip of St John's Lough.

As was the case on very many river navigations the presence of mills posed some tricky problems on the Ballinamore pro-ject. While Ballyduff cornmill was by then disused, the opposite was the case with the cornmills at Kilclare and Ballinamore and the corn and flour mills at Ballyconnell. The last-mentioned place was undoubtedly the most important, though there were difficulties over all three locations. Under section 30 of the 1842

D

Act the BOW was empowered to make necessary alterations to mills and mill works, provided that the water power was not reduced and that a statement of proposed alterations was made in the preliminary declaration. This power was granted for drainage improvements and where navigation was concerned it was extended greatly. The BOW could alter or remove mills and their works and in cases where the mill power could be improved with the owner's consent the latter could be charged for the works carried out.

On the Ballinamore works, however, the first dealings with the millers were less elaborate, the normal arrangement between them and the BOW being the stoppage of the mills for two weeks or a month in return for a sum of about £10 a week. During the stoppage as much work as possible would be carried out, as was the case at Ballyconnell in 1848–9 and at Ballinamore in 1849–50. The owner of the Ballyconnell mills was W. H. Enery who in May 1849 assented to the BOW offer to double the water power, partly at his cost, but the tenant was James Benison who received many hundreds of pounds in compensation over the years and who was involved in much argument with the BOW.

But the owner's assent was all that was required and Forsyth was instructed to go ahead with the work in July 1849. The BOW showed an awareness of the possibility of dispute in its instructions:

It is of great importance to run down the level of the waters above the mill, in order to excavate the shoals up to Skelan, and with this in view it is for you to consider whether you should either use a steam engine to work the mill, or else rent it for a year or such time as shall be necessary to effect the execution of the works.[21]

After some dispute the mill was stopped by agreement, the BOW paying compensation for the period except 'for any time there was enough water for the mill'. The agreed sum was £500, in return for which Benison would stop the flour mill from September 1849 for a year and the corn mill for September

1849 and again from March to September 1850, but the BOW
reserved 'a power to make further deduction for any time the
mills may be constantly supplied during the winter'. In the
event the final sum was £475 and the stoppage was used to
carry out the excavation of the shoals above Ballyconnell and
the alteration to the mill itself. By the end of 1850 its water
power had been trebled and two new water wheels had been
erected.

Alterations were also made in 1850 to the mill at Stradermot,
near Ballinamore. The head and tail race levels had been
altered by the navigation works and the mill machinery had to
be lowered by 4½ft—a process which bore fruit in January 1851
in the form of a notice of action against the BOW by the miller,
Charles Sharpley, who 'considered himself aggrieved by alterations made in his mill'.[22] The action was heard at the 1851
Leitrim summer assizes but was dismissed on a technical point.
An appeal was later made by Sharpley's widow and the case
dragged on for some years.

Eel fisheries also caused the odd headaches for the BOW. At
the start of the works arrangements were made to purchase the
eel weirs on the river at Garadice and Kilnacreevy and a total
of £222 was paid to the owners and tenants. There was also an
eel fishery at the old weir in Ballyconnell Demesne which was
removed early on in the works. In 1851 a plan was produced
for regulating sluices and an eel fishery in the demesne, it being
pointed out to Mulvany that 'although this work is an extra,
yet as it is to compensate for injury to the demesne and
especially for the loss of an eel fishery which would cost as
much or perhaps more, the expense therefore is approved
generally'. In carrying out the work Mulvany was warned

to guard against throwing up back-water on the regulating
weir and thus damaging the already precarious drainage above
Ballyconnell. There is also an important consideration as to the
making a free gap or Queen's share in such fishing weirs as
required by the fishery laws, which does not seem to be met by
your design.[23]

Modified or not, the plans were put into effect and the work virtually completed in 1852.

Despite the multitude of topics which had to be dealt with, the work—while very protracted and beset by a lack of funds— was not subject to all that much difficulty. Accidents to men were few and disputes were not too numerous, either involving the labourers or connected with the entry to and occupation of lands. In the latter case, however, the BOW had a handy weapon which could be produced to minimise delays. It was sanctioned by 9 Vic, c 4, s 41 and its title was self-explanatory —the 'Three-Day Notice'. In cases of difficulty over the occupation of land the BOW issued a notice, waited three days, and then went ahead, leaving the dispute to be sorted out later. This was a handy procedure and it was used for lands right along the canal though, happily, not very frequently.

Probably the darkest shadow on the proceedings was cast by the financial position, for as time went on it became clear that, for whatever reason, the estimates were hopelessly wrong. By the end of 1852, when the works were nowhere near completion, the expenditure stood at £173,969—a far cry from the estimated £131,858! It was then reckoned that £19,007 would be enough to complete the project, but time was to show that proportionately this was an even more ludicrous assessment of the situation.[24]

CHAPTER 4

# Protracted Progress
# (1853–60)

> The overexpenditure . . . will amount to near £50,000
> when the works on the Ballinamore & Ballyconnell
> Navigation are complete. I was not aware of this diffi-
> culty . . . I do not see my way out of it except by the
> application to Parliament for a grant in aid.
>
> *BOW Chairman, 1854*

AT the half-way stage in the construction the BOW did indeed
have big financial problems and there were periodic stoppages
of work as a result. Expenditure was racing ahead of the estimates and careful attention had to be paid to it. Part of the
difficulty arose from the separate accounting for the drainage
and navigation works. For example, in early 1854, while there
were abundant funds provided for the drainage, the navigation
account had only £13,000 which had not been appropriated.[1]
Economy was the keyword and the BOW had earlier asked
Mulvany anxiously 'can any part of the works . . . be omitted,
and what steps can be taken to hasten the closure of the expenditure on the District?'[2] Despite such efforts, however,
things got a little out of hand and in January 1854 the BOW,
replying to a query from the Treasury about the increase in
expenditure over an estimate of 1851, was forced to admit that
'it does not appear that any formal authority was transmitted to
the Board'.[3]

The position was not materially improved for over a year,
until the passing on 14 August 1855 of an Act which permitted

the 'Application of certain Sums granted by Parliament for Drainage and other Works of public Utility in *Ireland*, towards the Completion of certain Navigations undertaken in connexion with Drainages'.[4] One such navigation, of course, was the Ballinamore & Ballyconnell and the chances of its being completed improved considerably. The Treasury was empowered to cause alterations or curtailments of the schemes to be made and it could also reduce the portion of the cost to be charged on the counties concerned, any such amounts remitted to be considered as free grants. This was to benefit the district considerably. The Act also allowed the BOW to transfer, with Treasury consent, the completed navigations to the counties as their public property; previous Acts had stipulated that the BOW should retain control of the working navigations.

By the time of this Act, however, the BOW had already been compelled to take some drastic economy measures. At the meeting held on 13 November 1854 the BOW ordered:

> All the portions of the main channel for the navigation which have not already been completed to a greater depth than 4ft 6in below the proposed level of summer water in the reach are now to be dredged or excavated to that depth only—that is, to within 18 inches of the bottom level originally intended in all the reaches except that between Skelan and Aghoo Locks, and that between Ballyduff and Castlefore Locks, in which two reaches it has already been decided to raise the level of summer water 1 foot and to deepen the channel to within 2ft 6in of the bottom level originally intended.[5]

The reason for this latter change was the difficulty which Mulvany had been experiencing with the channel excavation in those reaches. Serious slipping of the banks had occurred and even to attain the reduced depth Mulvany thought that dredging would be necessary 'as there is much less likelihood of the bottom rising when the water is in the channel than when it is attempted to carry on the sinking by means of excavation within dams'.[6] The BOW ordered that the masonry of the locks and weirs concerned be 'carried out to suit the levels for which they were designed without any alteration' and this meant that the proposed raising of the summer level by a foot had to be effected by placing boards on the crests of the weirs at Skelan and Ballyduff. On the other hand, a few months previously the BOW authorised extra works on the new cuts for the Yellow and Aghacashlaun river diversions which would feed the navigation, so not all its moves were negative.

By this time, too, the BOW was knee-deep in matters which had hung fire from quite early on in the construction but which had to be dealt with sooner or later. The accounts for the re-built bridges—the 'county works'—had now to be taken care of. They were first forwarded for presentment at the 1852 Spring Assizes for Cavan and Fermanagh, but both counties had stalled, and the BOW declaration for Aghalane bridge met with such opposition that the matter was brought to a trial in March 1854. A deal of some sort was made, Fermanagh escaping with a charge of only £200, and the BOW, which had not been consulted, was annoyed, ordering its solicitor that 'in future no compromise of a legal process shall be effected by the legal advisers of the Board'.[7] The news of the unorthodox settlement with Fermanagh soon reached the ears of Cavan Grand Jury which by then was paying off its bill of £2,358 in four instalments and which thereupon sought and gained a reduction. The Leitrim declaration was sent to the 1856 Spring Assizes and payment was shortly afterwards made by the county. The totals charged on the counties were:

| | |
|---|---|
| Cavan | £1,910 |
| Fermanagh | £200 |
| Leitrim | £158. |

There was plenty of trouble over the mills, too. In late March 1854 at Ballyconnell 'part of the foundation and front wall of the cornmill gave way suddenly, carrying with it some of the new work'.[8] Prompt action was taken to repair the damage, the water being diverted from the mill from April until June—a necessary move which once again embroiled the BOW in a dispute with Benison. At Ballinamore there was trouble of another sort. After Charles Sharpley's action against the BOW in 1851 failed, the matter was kept alive by his widow, Bridget, whose claim that the mill had been injured by the alterations was brought to a hearing again early in 1853. To counter the charge Mulvany was told to 'take steps to secure the attendance of some respectable parties who can prove that the mill has been continuously at work since the completion of the works there'.[9] Before long, however, it was decided that purchase seemed the only way to resolve the difficulties for good and the BOW made a tentative inquiry whether £250 would buy the water power from the owner. In July 1854 the BOW decided that it was

> essential to purchase the mill and water power at Ballinamore and the water power of the mill at Kilclare in order to guard against an undue use of the water which may be required for the purposes of navigation in dry seasons, and to avoid the probability of future litigation with the owners of those mills.[10]

Under the terms of an Act of 1853 the matter was now referred to an arbitrator who would settle the terms of the transaction. W. P. Prendergast of Dublin was appointed, his brief being to arbitrate on the purchase money for

> the corn mill situate in the townland of Stradermot, parish of Oughteragh, and county of Leitrim, with water power belonging to said mill, together with the weirs, dams, and other works and obstructions to said mill and water power belonging or in anywise appertaining

and also for

> the water power of the mill situate in the townland of Kilclaremore, parish of Kiltubbrid, and county of Leitrim, commonly called and known as Kilclare Mill, together with the weirs, dams, obstructions and other works to said mill and water power belonging.[11]

It had been necessary to call in the arbitrator when the BOW inquiries met with exorbitant demands, and any lingering hopes that the matter would be smoothly dealt with were dispelled when the arbitrator's award for the Ballinamore mill was tra-

versed, the trial being held in July 1855. By the time the matter
was settled the BOW had paid £400 to the tenant, Mrs Sharpley,
and £700 to the estate of Catherine Penelope Jones of Maid-
stone, the owner of the water power—so much for the hopes
that £250 would suffice.[12] For the Kilclare water power the
purchase money came to £400, the mill itself being left to John
and Pat Doherty, its owners. They were allowed to use it for a
while in 1856 when the canal leaked to such an extent that the
mill could operate. In 1857 the leak was stopped and a notice
served on the Dohertys restraining them from using water
from the canal. This mill was to be used again some years later
but the Ballinamore mill was soon put to a quite different use.
The Belturbet workshop premises had been relinquished at the
end of April 1856 and soon afterwards the Ballinamore mill was
fitted up as a blacksmith's shop and store. The fittings were
removed for a time in 1857–8, when the dredgers for which
they were used were sent temporarily to the Lough Oughter
drainage district, but they were returned to the mill building
later in 1858.

The other big question still to be settled was that of 'the
purchase of the lands to be permanently retained for the works
of navigation', coupled to which of course was the compensation for temporary occupation and injury of lands. In order to
save time and smooth progress the BOW had from the outset
gone ahead with the works, leaving any arguments for later on.
The topic of land purchase was first given serious attention in
1852 and in November Samuel Gale was instructed to value the
lands to be purchased. Courts of inquiry were held at Carrick-
on-Shannon and Belturbet in March 1853 and at Ballyconnell
in June and October 1853. A sum of £8,588 was authorised to
be paid for lands taken or injured. While the courts allowed
many claims to be settled, other cases had to be referred to
arbitration, as provided for in the 1853 Act. The latter also
provided for the setting up of a standing committee of the
proprietors of a district to represent the landowners at arbitration proceedings and on 28 September 1853 the BOW gave

## Board of Public Works.

## DRAINAGE, NAVIGATION, &c.

### BALLINAMORE AND BALLYCONNELL DISTRICT.

# NOTICE

TO

# Railway and Bridge Contractors, Iron Founders, &c.

# TO BE SOLD BY AUCTION,

AT

# BELTURBET,

*in the County of Cavan,*

ON

### TUESDAY, the 2nd of SEPTEMBER, 1856.

THE Commissioners of Public Works have directed me to SELL by AUCTION the

## Plant, Tools, and Materials

which were in use on or provided for the Drainage and Navigation Works, and now Stored at BELTURBET, consisting of

## TWELVE SCREW PUMPS,

to which Horse-power can be applied, suitable for Unwatering Foundations for Bridge-building, and other large works, where effective Machinery is required.

Punching and Cutting Machine; Travelling Crane; Gantry Rails; Bellows; Anvils; Vices; Tongs; Grinding Stone; Windlasses; Trucks; Clay Picks; Crow Bars; Ringers; Sledges; Quarry and Stone Picks; Hammers; Jumpers; Scrapers; Rammers; Timber Carriage; Long Waggon; Pile Engine; Metal Shieves; Brasses; Spur Wheels; Hand Pumps;

and several other Articles of Machinery, Office Furniture, &c. Also, a quantity of Round and Flat Iron, a considerable portion of which is Lowmoor, of the best description; also, Angle and T Iron, Corrugated and New Scrap Iron; Cast Iron Scrap; Wrought Iron Scrap; Boiler Plate; Common Square Iron; a quantity of Chains and some Steel.

The Purchaser to pay 5 per Cent. Auctioneer's Fees.

### GEORGE CHADWICK,

*Auctioneer, Cavan.*

41. 8-56. 300—Printed by ALEX. THOM & SONS, 87, Abbey-street, Dublin.

FIG 5. Poster for an auction of surplus stores, 1856

notice of a meeting to be held to appoint such a committee for
the Ballinamore & Ballyconnell district. Francis Latouche of
Drumhierny was chairman of the committee subsequently
appointed but he does not seem to have been effective in getting
any action from his members for when the land arbitrations
began in autumn 1854 no members of the committee attended.
The first five cases were considered on 28 September and the
BOW later wrote to Latouche regretting the absence of the
committee and pointing out that the mill claims would shortly
come before the arbitrator and remarking that it feared 'that the
prices which the mill owners will seek to obtain will probably
be excessive'.[13] The BOW thought the committee should attend
for its own good—after all, according to 16 & 17 Vic, c 130, the
purchase money for the mills would be included in the charge
levied on the district. With or without the presence of the
standing committee members the arbitrations proceeded, with
some inevitable snags, and the problem of compensation was
more or less solved by the end of 1855, most payments having
been made in 1853–4.

While these formal proceedings were invaluable in dealing
with the larger claims there were still very many smaller ones
which had to be handled directly by the BOW and the correspondence flowed freely to and from its headquarters. There
were many disputes—Francis Reynolds was told in October
1853 that £5 would meet his claim, a letter noting 'you have
already been told that your holding could not be identified as
it was covered with spoil!'. Later on, the BOW told its engineer
to inform the Baxter family of Drumlogher that

the threatening tone of the letter in which they have thought
proper to address the Board . . . entirely precludes the possibility of the Board considering their claims for compensation . . .
You may add, however, that a request made in a different tone
may yet induce the Board to depart from the resolution they
have come to in the matter.[14]

Prompt atonement was evidently made for only a week later it
was agreed to pay £9 compensation. Cash payment was the

usual form of compensation, but at times a more practical approach was taken in places where the canal severed lands. Near Lough Scur a bridge was provided and at Dernagore Lord Erne's tenants were given a cot, or 'float', to ferry themselves to and fro across the new cut. Individual cash payments ranged from the £800 paid to the estate of Mrs Coulston to the 8s 6d (42½p) paid to Mrs C. Robinson.

While all these formalities were being dealt with work was continuing, even if at times fitfully, along the length of the navigation. Labour still proved difficult to obtain and the numbers at work fell steadily, although of course as progress was made the demand for men dropped. In 1853 work was still being done on the main channel, effort being concentrated on some difficult shoals. The following year saw a mammoth effort to clear a difficult stretch, advantage being taken of the stoppage of Ballyconnell mills for some repairs:

> The river at Skelan was completely closed by a dam, which had the effect of ponding up the water in Garadice Lake and the other lakes on the same level. By these means the reach of river-course between Ballyconnell and Skelan, about 5 miles in length, was run dry, or nearly so, and as many labourers as could be got at the time were set to remove any dams, unfinished portions of shoals, or deposit from the navigation and were so employed until the works at the mill were completed.[15]

Later in the year the mill was stopped by agreement with Benison to enable the work to be continued. Any work then remaining in this reach was left to the dredgers. The excavation had as usual been done by men with wheelbarrows and by 1855 all that could be done by this technique at any place had been done and thenceforth the main channel work was left to be completed by dredging.

In August 1853 the Belturbet-built steam dredger commenced work in the Aghalane sector and proved very effective in removing shoals and the remains of dams. It was then used to deepen the finished channel in appropriate places to the 4ft 6in summer depth required for navigation. In 1856 this dredger was called on to deepen the channel from Caroul Lock to Lough Erne by 4 inches, as during the previous summer the level of the Erne had fallen more than expected, leaving less than 4ft 6in depth along the northern stretch of the navigation. It was joined by another steam dredger in mid-1855. In May dredger 'C' from the Shannon Navigation was sent to work in the Ballinamore district and by the second week of June it was ready for work, making its way from Leitrim up to Castlefore. A year later 'C' was recorded as having reached Belturbet from Leitrim on 5 August—the first vessel of any size to go right along the navigation. Both dredgers were shortly afterwards sent to the Lough Oughter drainage district, not returning until June 1858. By then 'C' was in none too good condition and after much discussion it was sent away in April 1859 for re-boilering in Dublin. During the absence of the steam dredgers the hand-operated equipment was in great use, often at places where the steamboats had been at work but where slipping of the banks—and hence 'rising of the bottom'—had occurred. This trouble was to recur and more or less constant dredging was the only remedy for the problem and also in dealing with the deposition of silt and gravel particularly at the openings into the lakes, notably Garadice.

By the mid-1850s most of the major masonry works had been completed, the last road bridges constructed being those at Aghoo, Ballinacor and Derrygoan. However, quite a few accommodation bridges had yet to be erected across both drainage and navigation channels; among them were the bridges over the navigation at Derrymacoffin, Carrickmakeegan, Lisnatullagh, Cloncoohy and Derrinkip. Of Skelan it was reported in 1857 that

> the permanent footbridge and railing have been put over the weir to serve as a foot road, and to facilitate the raising and lowering of the regulating boards at the top of the weir.

Earlier that year there was quite a flurry over Aghalane bridge. Its summer headroom was 14ft 9in but at times of flood it could be reduced by as much as 9ft, whereas the flood-time headway elsewhere on the navigation was reportedly about 10ft. Evidently an objection was raised—possibly by J. G. V. Porter to whom the various figures had been quoted—for the BOW inquired into the question of rebuilding the bridge 'to prevent obstruction to the navigation'. However, it was soon decided to leave the bridge as it stood, possibly because it was thought that there would be little use of the navigation.

In 1856 the BOW had referred to the 'probable very limited amount of navigation', although Martin Farrell, who had succeeded Mulvany as engineer in charge, reported next year that 'the prospects of the value of the navigation to the country are becoming more apparent as the probability of opening it shortly becomes more generally known'.[16] This cautious optimism about the opening was in sharp contrast to the rash statements made some eight years earlier when it was claimed that the stretch from the Erne to Ballyconnell would be completed in summer 1850, the rest being ready in 1851. Now it was thought that in autumn 1857 the canal would be 'finally opened for traffic to the public'.

The principal stumbling block was the state of the navigation channel, for by 1856 the locks had at last been completed. The last job to be done was the fitting of the lock sluices. These were not ordered until 1854, when the directive was given to obtain 'lifting gear for sluices for locks . . . at the rate of £2 10s per set for the gearing to fit on loggerheads on the gates, and £4 per set for the gearing with cast iron casing, all to be delivered on board the [Ulster] canal boat at Caledon'.[17] The construction of the weirs at the eight river lock sites had kept pace more or less with the locks and by 1856 all had been built, and fitted with the large overflow sluices. Only the fish passes remained to be built and with two exceptions these were made in 1857.

One rather important matter which had been overlooked for a decade was dealt with in 1856—the building of lock houses. Tenders were sought in August for two toll collector's houses, one for either end of the canal, and six intermediate lock houses which were to be much smaller affairs. A month later the contracts were placed. Matthew Gardiner of Carrick-on-Shannon was awarded the contract for the collector's house at Caroul at £192 and for the six lock houses, for Ballyconnell, Skelan, Aghoo, Ballinamore, Castlefore and Lisconor, at £96 each, while that for the Killarcan (Leitrim) collector's house went to Andrew Curley of Carrick-on-Shannon at £173 10s. The houses were due to be completed by 1 July 1857 but bad weather and difficulties with the work on the foundations decreed otherwise. The latter factor resulted in Gardiner being authorised to carry out some extra work at a total cost of £65. At Caroul there was disagreement over the site of the house and the amount of land to be purchased from Lord Erne. The house there was undoubtedly the most awkwardly sited; it was on the island between the river and navigation channels, whereas all other houses were easily accessible. By summer 1858, however, all the houses were ready and the contracts paid for. Oddly enough, before the BOW had considered the question of providing for, let alone appointing, lock keepers local people were keeping an eye on potential jobs, and between 1854 and 1857 no fewer than 15 people applied for jobs, of whom 2 were ultimately appointed.

Among the matters still to be tidied up was the provision of a towpath. Although the original brief to John McMahon in 1844 had specified a navigation suitable for steamers and, indeed, the presence of the lakes made some sort of independent propulsion essential for boats, the BOW showed a curious insistence on having a towpath where practicable. In effect this meant that a towpath, fenced off from the adjoining lands, was made for most but not all of the way from Leitrim to Garadice Lake. In time most of the path was gravelled and provided with bridges over streams and drains and, in an early burst of enthusiasm, a towpath arch was even provided in Ballyconnell Bridge. Just east of Leitrim was a swampy region where there had been a small lake and in 1857 it was reported that 'the towpath has been formed across the Black Lough, and a covering of cross spars resting on split sleepers has been put on it'.[18]

Another task was the marking of 'the sailing course through certain lakes' and Farrell was told in 1856 that he would need 400 poles, many of which, of larch, were later delivered at Skelan and Aghoo. By 1857 'beacons' had been placed in the lakes and a year later Farrell stated that additional ones had been put up in Coologe, Derrycassan, Ballymagovern and Garadice lakes, and also in St John's Lough, 'to mark more particularly the course from one lake to another'. The BOW drew the line at anything not strictly necessary, however, and in 1858 told Farrell that his proposed 'wickerwork jetties at Garadice Lake' could not be approved, just as it had refused a request for a wharf at Ballinacor two years earlier.

The finishing of these smaller but none the less important matters was parallelled by other activity at board and parliamentary level. The 1855 Act had allowed for the handover of the completed works to the public ownership of the four counties concerned, and the procedure to be followed was spelt out even more clearly by an Act which was perhaps the most important of all—19 & 20 Vic, c 62, enacted on 21 July 1856. According to its provisions the BOW would decide which were navigation and which were drainage works and the latter would be described in an award and be henceforth given over to locally appointed drainage trustees who would maintain them, funding their efforts by a rate levied off the lands improved by the works. This was the basic procedure for all drainage districts, originally defined in 5 & 6 Vic, c 89, and only detail changes were made by later Acts. Thus for well over a century fifteen trustees of the Ballinamore & Ballyconnell Drainage District have been chosen by the proprietors at the triennial elections, and every year a programme of drainage maintenance works is carried out.

Under the 1856 Act the navigation works would also be formally described in an award of the BOW, and from the date of the award would vest in the Trustees for the Time being incorporated under this Act for such Navigation, for the use of the Counties, Baronies and Townlands chargeable under such Award, and shall be held, maintained, and preserved by such Trustees.[19]

Navigation trustees were a body corporate 'with perpetual succession and a common seal' and they were quite independent of drainage trustees—an arrangement which was to prove highly anomalous at times. The trustees representing a county could be removed by the appropriate grand jury which had the right to appoint successors. There was a qualification for membership of the navigation board, as it was commonly termed; everybody to be so elected

> shall be seised or possessed of Freehold or Leasehold Lands situate in the County on behalf of which he is elected of the yearly Value of One hundred Pounds or upwards over and above any Rent payable thereout, or shall be Agent to an Estate in such County of the yearly Value of Two thousand Pounds or upwards, or to Two or more Estates in such County of such yearly Value in the whole.[20]

There was nothing strange about this proviso at the time but it was to have serious consequences later on; likewise the stipulation that three trustees formed a quorum at meetings.

The Act named the persons who would be the first trustees of the Ballinamore & Ballyconnell Navigation District. There were twelve in all, three from each county, and as it was anticipated that the canal would be ready for handover very shortly it was ordained that they should hold their first meeting 'at Noon on the Third Tuesday in the Month of *January* next [1857] ... at the County Court House in *Cavan* in the County of *Cavan*'. An equally important purpose of the Act was to provide for the maintenance of the navigation once the trustees were in control. Section 25 was quite explicit:

> All Expenses of and incident to the Maintenance and Conservancy of each of the said Navigations shall (so far as the same may not be defrayed out of the Income aforesaid) be borne and paid by such Counties, Baronies, and Townlands, and Parts

E

thereof respectively, and in such Proportions as by the Award
of the said Commissioners of Public Works shall be in this
behalf provided.

The procedure was simple enough. The trustees had to send to
the grand juries at each spring and summer assizes an account
of their receipts and expenditure and they could also send along
an estimate of the amount necessary for the expenses of the
navigation for the next half-year. The trustees would calculate
their probable expenditure, deduct any sums in hand or owing
to them, and then pass a demand for the rest to the grand
juries, the amount being apportioned among the latter as laid
down in the navigation award. Once the counties received the
estimate they had to present the amounts sought without any
choice in the matter; not that in fact they did so without much
protest.

This Act applied to various navigations, but as far as the
Ballinamore Canal was concerned it was a little premature, for
over three years were to pass before the trustees took charge.
However, as legally bound to, they held their first meeting on
20 January 1857. Farrell was instructed to attend and to 'afford
every information which may be required of you except as
regards past expenditure'. Although no known records exist,
the trustees were apparently active enough, holding meetings
at intervals in spite of the fact that they had as yet no canal to
look after. In July 1858 they sought a meeting with Farrell to
discuss their fears about the state of the works. He referred the
request to Dublin and was quickly briefed:

> There can be no objection to your informing the Trustees of
> the Ballinamore District of the present condition of the works;
> but it is clearly out of the question that you should supply a
> critical statement—pointing out defects &c—which, it is
> apprehended, is what is required. You may inform the Trustees
> that upon the District being handed over to them a detailed
> description of the works, with plans, will be given to them.[21]

Possibly Farrell dispelled the trustees' doubts, for they were
not to correspond with the BOW again for nearly two years.

Meanwhile the finishing touches were being put to both the drainage and navigation works and at this time, too, the water-way saw the first of the small number of boats ever to use it. There is little concrete evidence about the trade boats using the canal, although there are records of permission to bring boats along it being granted to various people. In December 1856 the lock house contractor, Gardiner, was granted permission to use a boat, although he does not seem to have had one of his own. A little later, J. R. Tilson, the Ulster Canal Carrying Company's agent at Belturbet, was told that there was no objection to the 'trial trips proposed to be made at Ballyconnell'. In August 1857 Patrick Buchan, the tenant of the Creevelea ironworks and of coalpits in the Arigna region, was told he could 'pass a barge laden with coal through the junction canal'. A year later a Mr O'Donovan was likewise approved 'for the conveyance of timber from Ballyconnell to Belfast, provided he undertakes to defray any expense which may be incurred in working the lock [Caroul] and that he does not attempt to work it without having given due notice in order to secure the presence of an officer of the Board'.

According to Farrell there was an official trial on the canal in 1858:

In June, a trade-boat was hired from the Ulster Canal, and a load of tiles was brought from Florencecourt tilery to Ballyduff, near Ballinamore. After the delivery of the tiles a load of gravel was taken in at Ballyduff, which was brought to Leitrim. The boat was then taken to Lough Allen, and got a load of coals, which was brought to the steam dredger working at Garadice. It was worked by some of the canal ordinary workmen, and, although some heavy weather was encountered in Lough Allen, only four weeks elapsed between their leaving Crom with the tiles, and delivering the boat up to the Ulster Canal Company, including delivery of the tiles, taking in and delivering the gravel and coals.[22]

In October 1858 James Butler Pratt, the Leitrim county surveyor and a man later to become very closely connected with the canal, was given clearance to bring a screw streamer on to the canal. Although quite detailed arrangements were made for working through the locks, there is no certainty that a trip was made at that time.

However, there were definitely some trade boats on the canal around this time. Farrell stated that in December 1858

> a double turn in the canal, a little below Ballyconnell, was made wider, to prevent accident to the fan of the screw steamer, which, with the Board's permission, had been running between Carrick-on-Shannon and Belturbet since the previous month.[23]

This evidently continued for some time, for next April Farrell was told to report on 'the working of the Junction Canal by the Shannon Steam Navigation Company'. The Ulster Canal Carrying Company—or its successor the Dundalk Steam Navigation Company—also had a boat penetrate at least as far as Ballinamore, carrying 'a good deal of bread stuff'. The vessel in question, a 'steam lighter' with twin bow screws, was the TSS *Shamrock*, formerly owned by William Dargan. A steam yacht launched in mid-1858 by Denny of Dumbarton for the Earl of Erne also made its way along the canal to the Erne, although there is no formal record of its passage. Evidently other boats used the canal as well, for a request was made in April 1860 for permission 'to raise all the sluices at Skelan Lock to reduce the water' to allow a Mr Close 'to raise the boat, No 30, sunk in the canal'. The request was refused:

> This cannot be done. It would run off the water provided for the use of the navigation and Ballyconnell Mill; moreover it would take a long time to run down 1,400 acres to any extent and there might not be an opportunity of ponding such a quantity of water for some time to come.[24]

But the presence of even a few boats was sure evidence that the waterway was virtually complete and that the district was ready for handover to the trustees. The BOW had to make its award as soon as the navigation 'shall have been completed in such Manner and to such Extent as shall be directed or approved of by the Commissioners of Her Majesty's Treasury'.

Such an award would specify the costs of the works and the portion which would be charged on the carefully defined district; it would also set out the mode of repayment of this sum. For the drainage district the BOW would also draw up an award which specified the works, their cost, the portion of improved land belonging to each proprietor and the portion of the charge payable by each owner, the proportion of future maintenance charges to be borne by each proprietor, and the amount which would be levied for the first year's maintenance.

The draft awards had then to be printed, published and deposited for inspection, notice being given that objections should be lodged within a specified time. The next stage was a meeting at which objections would be heard, alterations made to the drafts if necessary, and finally the awards signed by members of the BOW. The signed documents—the final awards—would be enrolled in chancery and become conclusive. This procedure, of course, entailed much work for the BOW and it began the lengthy process in 1857, calling on Farrell to make a careful inspection of both the drainage and navigation districts 'as to their state and fitness to be given over to the trustees'. Later he was told to have detailed plans prepared showing full details of the works, and shortly afterwards Brassington was instructed to make the valuation which would provide the data necessary for the drainage award. Letters were also collected from doctors in the region confirming that the drainage works had improved the general sanitary condition of the area. Forsyth was sent back to the district to make an inspection in September 1858 and to report what further works would be needed before handover.

The Treasury, which would instruct the BOW on the financial aspects of the award, was also interested in the district and its Commissioners of Special Inquiry were investigating the works by February 1859. Their report was signed on 15 July 1859 and it showed that the expenditure up to the previous 25 June, exclusive of the £2,268 repaid for the county works, had been:

| Drainage | £48,340 |
|----------|---------|
| Navigation | £224,460 |
| Mill Power | £1,472 |
| | £274,272 |

representing an excess of £140,942 over the original estimate.[25] The inquiry commissioners recommended that the landowners whose property was improved by the drainage works, although liable to pay £27,110, should pay the slightly reduced sum of £25,500 in instalments with interest at 4 per cent per annum. Concerning the navigation, the report continued:

the proportion of the expenditure for which the district set forth in the declaration is legally responsible amounts to one half. The prospects of advantage, however, and of a remunerative return which the project was originally considered to hold out, have, we believe, been materially interfered with and lessened by the altered circumstances of the country at large and the general extension of railways. That mode of conveyance has not yet, however, been brought immediately within reach of the district in question, and we believe that the actual benefit which the district may still derive from the junction canal under energetic management would justify us in recommending that that the moiety of the original estimate, vizt £49,625, should be required to be repaid, but considering that a portion of the canal has not been completed to the full depth and that a sum of £5,000 would probably yet be required to do so, and looking to the limited extent of the district made liable, and the amount of the rate which will be required to be levied in repayment, we have to submit that the charge should be limited to £30,000, and that the Commissioners of Public Works be accordingly authorised by their Lordships, under the provisions of the Act 18 & 19 Vic, c 110, to prepare an award for that amount, and as we are advised that no interest is legally chargeable in consequence of deferred payment, we have further to recommend that the period for such repayment be limited to five years.

Some five years previously the BOW was worried over the exact liability of the district—was it for one half the originally estimated cost, to which assent had been given by the grand juries, or was it for one half the actual cost? As the chairman

wrote to the Treasury, the question was one which 'I appre-
hend will be fought—think of our friend Roscommon'. This
last reference is the first indication that the Roscommon Grand
Jury had become distinctly uneasy about a canal which would
bring the most indirect benefits at best. The opinion was that
the counties were liable to pay half the actual cost, but one
BOW member noted that 'there do not appear to be any
grounds *now* for expecting that the counties will consider
themselves bound for the repayment of any excess of estimate'.[26]

The inquiry commissioners' comments on railway development were valid enough in that the spread of railways very
much reduced the need for a Limerick–Belfast navigation, as
had been envisaged, but the usefulness of the canal for local
trade would not be affected at all. None the less their remarks
have been widely misquoted, the impression being given that
direct railway competition killed the canal. The final recommendations of the commissioners concerned the mill at Ballyconnell; it was suggested that a charge of £750 be made on the
proprietor and included in the drainage award.

At the beginning of August 1859 the report was deposited
with the clerks of the peace of the four counties, to await
objections which were to be made before 13 September. Six
weeks later the draft awards were lodged for public inspection
and shortly afterwards the maps of the district were lodged in
the lock house at Ballinamore. The award meeting at which
objections would be considered was arranged for 10 January
1860 at the Courthouse, Ballinamore. By late 1859 Forsyth had
reappeared on the scene to replace Farrell, who had died, and
he was ordered to attend the meeting, having made a report
immediately beforehand on the work remaining to be done.
The three overseers of the works along the canal would also
attend, while the BOW would be represented by two of its
members and its solicitor. Orders were also given for the sur-
render of the offices and stores in the district so that no further
expense would be incurred once the awards had been signed.

In the weeks before the meeting objections were coming in

from landowners concerning the valuations in the draft award and from others concerning the works. There were requests from some proprietors that the meeting be transferred to Ballyconnell and it was decided in advance to adjourn the meeting in Ballinamore on 10 January and to resume next day in Ballyconnell. Accordingly, the objections concerning lands west of Ballinamore were segregated for the first day's proceedings.

The meeting was held as planned and so, on 10 January 1860, two BOW members signed and sealed the final award for the Navigation District of Ballinamore and Ballyconnell, and the navigation was vested in the trustees appointed nearly four years earlier. The financial details were clearly set out—the navigation works had cost £228,651 10s 5d (£228,651.52) inclusive of interest, of which all but £30,000 would be deemed a free grant. The £30,000 was to be repaid by ten half-yearly instalments, the respective county burdens being

| County | Total charged | | Proportion of whole |
|---|---|---|---|
| Cavan | £10,029 12s | (£10,029.60) | 0.33432 |
| Fermanagh | £ 2,550 18s | (£ 2,550.90) | 0.08503 |
| Leitrim | £12,720 6s | (£12,720.30) | 0.42401 |
| Roscommon | £ 4,699 4s | (£ 4,699.20) | 0.15664 |
| | £30,000 | | 1.00000 |

The proportions were very important, for the award confirmed that future levies for maintenance would be apportioned in exactly the same way on a specified list of townlands which were set out in a very lengthy appendix. A second schedule listed the works which were to be maintained 'as works of Navigation' by the navigation trustees (see page 147).

The drainage award was not settled on this occasion, however, as some objections to valuations were upheld and referred back to Brassington. The BOW recommended to the Treasury that the £25,500 charge suggested by the inquiry commissioners be reduced to £24,412 and it was this sum which was ordered to be charged over 22 years with interest at 4 per cent by the 'Drainage & Water Power' award which was signed and made final on 6 March 1860. This award confirmed the Ballyconnell mill charge as £750, to be repaid in like manner.

Once the awards were made final there were relatively few formalities left. Certificates for the county charges for the navigation were prepared and sent out on 20 February 1860. On 3 April a notice was sent out summoning proprietors to a meeting at Ballyconnell on 15 May to elect the first trustees of the drainage district. Once that meeting was held and appointments made the BOW would be more or less free of responsibility for the drainage district. There was some little delay, however, in disposing of the navigation. In February 1860 the BOW asked the Treasury to sanction formally the issue of the necessary warrant by which the transfer of the navigation to the trustees would be made. On 16 March the secretary of each of the four grand juries was sent a copy of the warrant

> directing that the Ballinamore & Ballyconnell Navigation with the tolls thereof shall become the public property of the counties in which the lands chargeable under the Award of the Commissioners [of Public Works] are respectively situate.[27]

The BOW wrote to the trustees on 28 April asking that they appoint someone to receive 'the maps and plans, keys of the collectors' and lock-keepers' houses, and such portions of the moveable gearing in connection with the locks &c., as it may be necessary to take into special charge, on some day not later than the 22nd of May next'. There was no reply and one had to be sought a fortnight later. Still no reply came and the BOW wrote on 13 June to say that it could not 'longer defer giving over to the Trustees the works of navigation'. Unless someone was appointed the BOW would have no choice but to withdraw the few persons remaining as caretakers. The trustees met a fortnight later and appointed James Butler Pratt as their engineer and secretary. He was asked by the BOW to take charge on or before 4 July, on which date all its personnel would be withdrawn. This time the pleas were answered and on 4 July 1860 the navigation finally passed out of the hands of the Commissioners of Public Works.

# CHAPTER 5

# A Sorry Affair (1860–80)

The present inutility of the canal may be ascribed in
great measure to the state in which it was transferred to
the counties.

*Crichton Committee, 1878*

THE trustees got down to serious business on 27 June 1860,
perhaps when they had decided that further delaying tactics
were pointless. The meeting, like most others, was held in
Dublin and secretary/engineer Pratt had to travel up from
Leitrim, receiving his expenses. He was ordered to obtain a seal
for the use of the trustees. A week later Pratt took charge of the
canal from the BOW and on the very day of the handover—4
July—he submitted a report on its condition to the board and
made application for a loan of £800 for two years' maintenance.
The BOW acknowledged the report without comment and
pointed out that under s 26 of 19 & 20 Vic, c 62 he should ask
the Treasury for a loan of £500 for one year's maintenance.
This he did, and at the beginning of August the desired advance was made by the Treasury on the recommendation of the
BOW.[1]

Letters on various topics flowed from the BOW to Pratt, one
of 20 July stating that the BOW had sold hay along the banks
for several seasons past and recommending that the trustees
should continue the practice, it being 'very desirable' that it
should be done 'for the sake of preventing parties establishing
claims by rights of usage'. Another, dated 5 December, referred
to the trustees' suggestion that suitable mill sites might be let;

78

it stated bluntly (and correctly, according to 20 & 21 Vic, c 23):

> No water power or mill site in connexion with the navigation [is] vested in the trustees and they have therefore no power of making any such letting as referred to.[2]

This did not impress the trustees, who ignored the statement and placed a series of newspaper advertisements which proclaimed the opening of the canal, offered to lease the tolls (unsuccessfully), and announced the intention to lease the 'water power and several mill sites' on the canal (almost equally unsuccessfully).

That was in January 1861, and in June the BOW replied to Pat Doherty of Kilclare, who offered £5 a year for the right to work his corn mill:

> the navigation is now in the hands of trustees, who have no power to grant your request, neither would the Board sanction it as they have previously informed you.[3]

Undeterred, Doherty made a deal with the trustees in September and for £5 a year won the 'right' to take water for his mill from the canal. The agreement ran until 1873 and the rental dropped to £3 in 1867. In all the trustees received £48 from the Kilclare miller—a sum which when supplemented by the rental of the spoil banks along the canal (the trustees took the BOW advice on this point!) far exceeded the amount received in tolls.

Tradition, apparently based on a statement by Robert Manning in 1881, holds that only 8 boats ever used the canal while it was officially open. This is certainly an underestimate, as there are indications that tolls were paid on eight occasions—giving a grand total of something over £18 as the maximum sum received for traffic on a navigation costing almost £¼ million! This was in the period 1862–7, outside which other boats are known to have passed, apparently toll-free. Pratt claimed years later that he had brought a boatload of coal from Arigna to Enniskillen, using a borrowed steamer, but this may have been before 1860 and not in 1861 as he recalled. In 1868 the SS

## BALLINAMORE AND BALLYCONNELL NAVIGATION.

NOTICE IS HEREBY GIVEN, that this navigation, 39 miles in length; is now open for Public Traffic connecting the River Shannon, near Carrick-on Shannon with Lough Erne and the North of Ireland. The locks are constructed to pass a Steamer 82 feet long, and 16th feet beam, drawing 4½ feet water.

The Trustees are now prepared to let on lease or otherwise, as may be agreed on, under their Act of Incorporation, the Tolls and Rates of this Navigation. and also the WATER POWER AND SEVERAL MILL SITES on same.

For further particulars, apply to
JAMES B. PRATT,
Engineer to Trustees, Co. Surveyor's Office,
Drumsna, County Leitrim.
January 23, 1861.

FIG 6. The first advertisement soliciting traffic, 1861

*Knockninny*, built in Dublin for the Erne, was brought along the canal; she was owned by J. G. V. Porter, a son of one of the trustees, and possibly on this account no tolls were charged. By the time the last boat passed, by 1873 at the latest, the trustees had lost interest in tolls. This last vessel was W. R. Potts's carvel-built yacht *Audax* which went from the Erne to the Shannon.[4] But whatever the precise number of boats it seems certain that the total for the years from 1860 onwards cannot have exceeded a pathetic fifteen.

One thorny question first arose in January 1861 and it was to recur many times—the maintenance of the wooden accommodation bridges over the navigation. It was referred by Pratt to the BOW which replied that it was

unwilling to give [its] opinion on a legal point for the guidance of the trustees but would refer them to the Navigation Award, and the Schedule B referred to therein, as to the bridges to be maintained.[5]

This was a neat evasion of the issue, as a study of the drainage and navigation awards—separate documents which *should* have been independent—leads to the conclusion that the navigation award, prepared first, was drawn up in a hurry and that the BOW belatedly realised this and tried to tie up any loose ends in the later drainage award. Certainly the navigation works are defined much more fully in the drainage award which also revealed that the maintenance of the accommodation bridges across the navigation channel was the responsibility of the drainage trustees! Generally, both bodies of trustees took the line that if a feature needing repair was mentioned in their award they would undertake the job, otherwise not. The loose terminology of the award schedules which set out the works did not help matters at all. Relevant extracts from these schedules are given in Appendix 4; they are worthy of study.

Pratt and the BOW were also in correspondence on the topic of byelaws for the navigation and in June 1861 the latter received a copy of the proposed regulations. The BOW pointed out that the approval of a judge was necessary 'which does not appear to have been given or applied for by the trustees',[6] while the Treasury had to approve the proposed schedule of tolls, which they did in July. The byelaws were considered for some months and were finally approved at a meeting in December. Soon afterwards they were printed. Unfortunately no details of the tolls or byelaws are known to survive.

On the conclusion of the construction work the BOW, doubtless realising from experience that much clearing of the channel would be needed in future, decided to hand over to the trustees the Belturbet-built steam dredger along with two barges, an anchor boat and a heterogeneous collection of planks, chains and ironwork, without which it was felt that 'the future maintenance of the works cannot be duly attended to'. The conditions of the proposed transfer were that the items be maintained and retained and to this the trustees agreed on 27

BALLINAMORE and BALLYCONNELL
NAVIGATION DISTRICT.
N O T I C E.
NOTICE IS HEREBY GIVEN, that t' e Right Honourable
BARON DEASY will hold a MEETING at 12 o'clock noon,
On the 20th day of DECEMBER 1861,
at No 27 MERRION SQUARE NORTH, in the CITY OF
DUBLIN, to take into consideration the Bye-Laws made by
the Trustees of this Navigation; and to hear any objections
that may be made to same.
  And Notice is also Given, that copies of said Bye-Laws and
copies of this Notice, have been deposited for inspection with
the Clerks of the Peace, Clerks of the Poor Law Unions, and
Clerks of the Petty Sessions Districts comprised in this Navigation District.
                          JAMES B. PRATT,
                  Secretary and Engineer to the Trustees
                     of the Ballinamore and Ballyconnell
                          Navigation District.
  Drumsna, 26th November 1861.

FIG 7. Notice for the byelaws meeting, 1861

June 1860. They soon found out, however, that the boats—not
least the dredger—were in bad condition and they wrote to the
BOW on the question of repairs. The reply was distinctly
unhelpful:

> In regard to the dredging machinery the Board have to remind
> Mr Pratt that it was a free gift to the district from Her Majesty's
> Treasury.[7]

After having spent £38 on the 'gift' the trustees decided to
reject it on 26 January 1861 and they resolved:

> that application be made to the Board of Works to take into
> their possession the hand and steam dredgers which are con-
> sidered expensive and useless to the Trustees.[8]

The BOW agreed to take them back but the steam dredger
posed a problem as it had sunk at Ballinamore. It was raised in
May and brought to the Shannon where it lay idle for most of
the time until 1869 when it was scrapped.

  Notwithstanding all the correspondence there was one major
topic on which the BOW was amazingly silent—the condition
of the navigation. While Pratt had indicated right at the outset

that its condition was, to say the least, rather less than perfect, he was not aware just how bad the position was. The trustees made a serious mistake in not commissioning long before they took control the survey which Pratt made in autumn 1860. He made a detailed report in October and it was a fascinating document. It first described the canal, noting that the summit level was 79ft above the Shannon at Leitrim (reached through 8 locks with an average lift of 9ft 10½in), and 66ft above the level of the Erne (each of the other 8 locks having an average lift of 8ft 3½in). It then turned to the depth of water which was originally intended to be 6ft:

> The works have been executed for a depth of only four and a half feet, and this depth . . . has not been carried out, as there are parts of the navigation not more than three and a half feet deep, unless when the water is kept up by putting a board on the weir walls. The water in the lakes between Castlefore and Ballyconnell is kept about two feet higher than the level proposed by Mr McMahon in his original report and plans, and this is done in order to keep four and a half feet of water on the shallows of these lakes, which shallows . . . were to be removed . . . When there are six feet of water on the lock of Castlefore, the shallows in Lough Scur, the summit level, vary, from four to five feet, and in dry weather, in summer, the supply to the summit level is not sufficient to maintain the water at this height, the leakage through the lock and weir at Castlefore and through the banks and lock No 9, at Kilclare, reduce the water about sixteen inches.[9]

This was perhaps the most serious complaint but the thorough Pratt continued with a catalogue of other defects—the banks were too steeply sloped and were giving way 'and have caused a deposit of mud in some places two feet deep'; the fencing was 'entirely defective'; the towpath was badly made; some of the locks were ill-made and most of them leaked considerably 'through the joints of the masonry'. The locks at Skelan, Castlefore and Kilclare, in particular, were very bad. Indeed, at Kilclare 'the leakage through the bank and lock No 9 is so considerable that the waste water is sufficient to turn Kilclare Mill the whole year'. The lock houses were built of 'badly burnt and unsound brick' and were 'crumbling down with the weather'. The 'approaches to most of the bridges, as at Newbrook, Kilclare and Aghoo' had subsided while all the wooden bridges were badly made and 'not safe for traffic'. The old bridge at Derrygoan made of stone had been replaced by a wooden structure which was now 'in a dangerous state'. Pratt also commented on the sluices erected at the weirs on the eastern section of the waterway; they were not self-acting and were 'very troublesome to attend to in floods', a fact which in the case of Caroul at least had been realised before the handover. His remarks on the dredging machinery were likewise on the caustic side.

Pratt wound up his list of complaints with a firm statement as to where the responsibility for making good the defects lay.

> It is evident, from the foregoing, that traffic cannot be carried on except by small steamers, and that the works now necessary to make the navigation available, and protect the public, should not come under the head of repairs, but as works necessary to open and complete the navigation, as all the works now required were wanting before the canal was given over to the trustees.

The report, along with a detailed estimate of the 'expense of finishing and repairing the several works above referred to, which estimate amounts on the whole to £1,718', was sent off to the BOW which made only the briefest reply, its secretary being instructed:

> Inform Mr Pratt that the Board cannot undertake the repairs which it is the duty of the trustees to perform at the cost of the district, of which the navigation is the property.[10]

Thereupon Pratt's detailed report was pigeon-holed and it was to lie unseen and unpublished for over 15 years.

And so it was up to the trustees themselves to do something about their woebegone navigation. While they could have contented themselves with keeping the works in the precise state in which they received them, this would not have improved

*Page 85* Weirs: (*above*) the broken weir at Caroul; (*below*) the crest of Ballyduff weir, showing the remains of the mountings for the flash boards

Page 86  Houses: (*above*) rear view of Ballyconnell lock house; (*below*) the ruinous toll collector's house at Killarcan

their chances of earning anything from boats and so they set out
to carry out what repairs they could with the £500 borrowed
from the Treasury, a sum supplemented by the amounts levied
off the counties. However, it was apparent even at this early
stage that to obtain money from the counties, Acts notwithstanding, would never be the easiest of procedures. Roscommon was the first to baulk and early in 1860 a memorial was
sent to the Treasury praying that

> the Barony of Boyle in the County of Roscommon may be re-
> lieved from the charge imposed on it in respect of the naviga-
> tion between the Shannon and the Erne.[11]

It was referred to the BOW which made the telling point that
the region was specified in the 1847 declaration and continued:

> The first instalment of the charge certified for pursuant to [the
> Final] Award has also been presented for by the Grand Jury of the
> county, by or on behalf of whom, or by any person concerned,
> no representation was made when the opportunity was given,
> and the Board are advised that their Lordships [of the Treasury]
> are not now empowered to cancel any part of that Award.[12]

An attempt was made in summer 1860 to block the payment of
the sum presented by Roscommon Grand Jury but it proved
unsuccessful and the amount was paid along with subsequent
ones. The other counties also paid off their share of the capital
charge along with the periodical maintenance levies but the
trustees had to engage a solicitor to apply pressure at times.

The trustees first tackled the maintenance of the locks. Then
they had the fences and bridges attended to. While the work
was commencing the advertisement placed by the trustees was
meeting with absolutely no response from boat owners, who
seemingly avoided the canal completely. For a few years, however, the trustees pressed on with their maintenance but they
then began to have doubts, or as Pratt later put it 'they began
to think it was no use'. They decided to make a final attempt to
attract boats. A second, rather longer advertisement was placed
in eleven newspapers even more widely dispersed throughout

F

# Ballinamore and Ballyconnell Navigation District.

## Act 19th and 20th Victoria, chap. 62.

THE Trustees of this Navigation District, pursuant to the above Act, are prepared to Let on Lease, on such Terms as may be agreed on, the Rates and Tolls of Canal, called the "Ballinamore and Ballyconnell Navigation," commencing on the River Shannon, near Carrick-on-Shannon, and terminating in Lough Erne. It connects the Shannon Navigation and the South of Ireland, with the Ulster and Newry Canals on the North ; and joins the Coal Mines and Iron Mines, and Gypsum Quarries of the Lough Allen District, with the several water communications in the North and South of Ireland.

This Canal is 38 miles in length, and is suited for small Steam Vessels ; each Lock is 82 feet long and 16 feet wide.

The Towns of Carrick-on-Shannon, Boyle, Drumshanbo, Ballinamore, Ballyconnell, Belturbet, and several other small Towns, calculated to produce a profitable trade, are in this District. The Lough Erne Steam Company's splendid steamer now plies daily on the Lakes.

The Trustees will entertain, on most Liberal Terms, any application from Parties willing to develope the Traffic of this extensive and improving District.

For further information apply to

JAMES B. PRATT,
Engineer to Trustees,
County Surveyor's Office, Drumsna,
County Leitrim.

June 23.

FIG 8. The second and last unsuccessful advertisement, 1864

the country in mid-1864. But again there was no response and from then on thoughts of maintaining the waterway in a fit state for boats began to recede. However, there was no definite decision to abandon the navigation as such and to concentrate solely on maintenance of the channel and works for drainage purposes only. It has been stated quite authoritatively at times that such a decision was taken in 1865, but repairs to locks— sometimes extensive as at Ballyduff and Skelan in 1867—were being carried on as late as 1871. In the latter year the first known contract for the clearing of mud and debris from the channel was granted to Charles Gill, the toll collector at Killarcan, and this set the pattern of most later maintenance works.

Notwithstanding this maintenance the condition of the canal was definitely on the decline, as evidenced by the experience of J. G. V. Porter when he brought the *Knockninny* along the canal from the Shannon late in 1868.

> Only through the kindness of the people, and Mr Pratt, the engineer, was I able to get through the canal. They took the greatest trouble to get water from one reach to another to float me down. But my coming through it is no proof [of its navigability] for it took me three weeks to get through.[13]

If that was the case in 1868 things must have been very much worse some five years later when the *Audax* made its voyage from Erne to Shannon. One could not blame the trustees for running down and eventually ceasing their maintenance of purely navigation works. The passage of a decade with about a dozen boats had shown beyond question that no one was interested in the link—the growth of railways had apparently taken care of that—while there turned out to be no local traffic to warrant the retention of the waterway.

None of the hopes for the revival of the Arigna mining district had been realised and by the early 1860s the latest industrial venture in Leitrim, the Creevelea iron works, was also at a standstill. While there was some development of the mining region some twenty years later it came far too late for the canal to derive any benefit from it. The trustees had the express support of at least one of the grand juries, though doubtless all four would have been happy to see maintenance cut back with a consequent reduction in levy demands. As soon as it had discharged the last of its share of the capital charge Cavan Grand Jury resolved at the 1865 spring assizes that

> they desire to express their unanimous sense of the utter inutility of this navigation, and they earnestly hope that the Commissioners of Public Works will not continue to exercise the power, vested in them, of obliging the trustees of this navigation to maintain (save so far as may be necessary for drainage purposes) any of the works connected with this navigation, which have now been in operation for some years, and have been fully proved to be totally valueless to this county, which has been so heavily taxed for it.[14]

From the early 1870s the navigation was being neglected and it deteriorated seriously. Admittedly, the lock keepers were to continue in office for some years, receiving their meagre wages. But they had little to do and, east of the summit level, their principal task was the regulation of flood waters by proper control of the large weir sluices. Maintenance work was curtailed and effort concentrated on keeping the main channel reasonably clear as a drainage artery. That was the extent to which the trustees would go and all the evidence indicates that in the mid-1870s they adopted a policy which would lead to a showdown and bring matters out into the open.

As Cavan Grand Jury had indicated, the BOW had a function in regard to the maintenance of the canal though it was not quite as the wording of the resolution implied. Under s 29 of 19 & 20 Vic, c 62, if a memorial from five or more ratepayers in a navigation district was sent to the Lord Lieutenant alleging that the works were not being maintained properly by the trustees the matter could be referred to the Treasury, which in turn would refer it to the BOW for a statement of the necessary repairs and their estimated cost. If the trustees declined to carry out the repairs the Treasury would grant funds to the BOW to have the work done. On its completion a certificate of the amount would be furnished to the Lord Lieutenant who would then signify to the appropriate grand juries the baronies and townlands to be charged with the cost. As far as the ratepayers were concerned they paid for the works whether they were executed normally by the trustees or as a result of such a memorial. In the latter case, however, the charge could be apportioned on quite a small area, causing a high rate, and so the inclination of people to send memorials seeking works which might be desirable but not essential was dampened somewhat.

Doubtless because the trustees were sitting tight two memorials were made to the Lord Lieutenant early in 1875 and in time found their way to the BOW. One was from 'the rate-payers of the barony of Tullyhaw, county of Cavan' for the repairs of 'an embankment, weir, lock gate and sluice' at Bally-connell, the condition of which was such that the mills were without a water supply.[15] These repairs were indeed essential and the fact that they were not undertaken by the trustees who would have been aware of this fact is strongly suggestive of their deliberate inertia. The second memorial came from 'the ratepayers of the county of Leitrim, for the repairs of the navigation from the Shannon to Ballinamore'. Both were referred to Robert Manning, the BOW chief engineer, for a report and in May 1875 the Treasury was informed that the repairs at Ballyconnell would cost £130. The estimate was approved and plans were made to have the work put in hand. Specifications were ready in September but there was difficulty in getting a contractor and in the long run it was James Lang, the miller, who after much haggling was awarded the £130 contract in August 1876. The memorialists were all too aware of the levy they would have to bear, for they declined to take up a BOW suggestion that the work be done more promptly but more expensively. A certificate for the cost was sent to the Lord Lieutenant in January 1877 and the amount presented at the Cavan spring assizes that year.[16]

Prompted by the other memorial Robert Manning duly

examined the canal from Ballinamore westwards, estimating the cost of its restoration at £4,400 in his report of 10 June 1875. The report was passed to the Lord Lieutenant with the views of the BOW:

> As this navigation has never been made use of since handed over to the trustees, representing the counties of Cavan, Leitrim, Fermanagh and Roscommon, through which it passes [sic], and as the outlay of so large a sum as Mr Manning's estimate would impose a heavy charge on the county of Leitrim, the Commissioners think it would be desirable that the views of the trustees should be ascertained before further steps be taken.[17]

The matter was referred to the trustees, passed back with suitably critical comment, and again referred to the BOW which gave its final opinion:

> The prospects of any trade arising on the navigation, or of any benefits to the surrounding districts therefrom, are not such as would appear to warrant the expenditure estimated at £4,400.

That ended all talk of restoring the waterway and the decline went on uncontrolled, by now uninterrupted by any maintenance activity. For by 1876 the trustees had more or less decided to cease operations. In 1877 most of the lock keepers received their last pay and those still nominally on the payroll would not receive any further remuneration for many years. The last rents had been collected from the tenants of the spoil banks some years earlier, and the last trustees' meeting known to have been held at this period took place at the Hibernian Hotel in Dublin on 26 April 1878 when, presumably, they decided to call it a day. Certainly, there now began a period of inactivity during which no maintenance was carried out, no rents were collected nor wages paid, and no meetings were held, while along the canal the works fell into disrepair.

But the waterway was not forgotten—not by a long way. Within three years it would be discussed at length before two inquiries and its sorry history well publicised. First of these was a Committee of Inquiry into the activities of the BOW, appointed by the Treasury and with Viscount Crichton as its chairman. Some very interesting evidence was given at the hearings in late 1877 and one of the first witnesses to be examined was the then BOW chairman, Colonel J. G. McKerlie, who had signed both awards and who had been very much involved in the project. His main concern at the early stage of the inquiry was in maintaining that the trustees were fully aware of the condition of the canal before the award had been made final. He pointed out that no objections had been made at that stage. The poor colonel was later back in the limelight again after some colourful evidence had been given by one of the trustees, the articulate John Grey Vesey Porter of Belleisle, of whom it was later remarked that he was 'almost crazy on the subject of reopening the canal'.

Porter was mainly concerned about the failure of interested parties to have an inquiry held into the state of the Ballinamore Canal. Fermanagh Grand Jury, which appointed him as a trustee, had at recent assizes passed 'two strong resolutions' seeking a Government inquiry, something which the trustees themselves had unsuccessfully sought in 1875. To Porter the reasons were clear enough.

> Here is a report of the Commissioners of Inquiry . . . in 1859, into this very canal, and what do I find? At page 8 the signatures of Richard Griffith and J. G. McKerlie, Special Commissioners of Inquiry into the Drainage of Ireland; and at page 13 there is a report, signed by the same Richard Griffith and J. G. McKerlie, as Commissioners of Public Works. The same two men sitting at Cavan in one capacity, and pretending to inquire into their own acts, are sitting in Dublin in another capacity. There is a specimen of the manner in which public business is done in Ireland.[18]

Porter expanded on his theme and made one quite serious charge, that in effect those to be charged under awards were blackmailed, to put it bluntly.

What I wish to show to this Committee is that then, in 1859, in consequence of general complaints from Ireland against the mismanagement, failures, under-estimates, and over-costs of the Board of Works, a special inquiry was appointed, and that inquiry was made a farce by the Government, which made its Commissioners the Board of Works themselves, to examine into their own mistakes; and also I wish to show that the reason in 1859 that those inquiries were not pushed further by the landlords who complained, is that they were afraid that, if so, less sums would be remitted from the amounts legally charged against them.[19]

On the question of the state of the canal Porter commented that the trustees were wrong in accepting charge from the BOW 'merely on their statement that it was duly finished, and without any competent and independent inquiry'. This omission, he felt, was 'the principal cause of all this trouble'.

Col McKerlie was re-examined and he had a shot at rebutting Porter's evidence, but his plaintive claim that 'there was a connexion of a navigable character when the works were completed' could hardly have cut much ice with the committee. He produced Pratt's report of October 1860 and it was revealed that this was the first time it had been made public and there had been no rebuttal of it. In reply to a question as to his opinion on the state of the canal he said:

It was not handed over certainly as well as could have been desired, but, looking at the vast expenditure which had been incurred, the large amount remitted, and the little prospect of its being of any practical use, we did not think that we would be justified in expending further money upon it.[20]

Yet, as he had stated earlier, lock houses had been built as late as 1857, having been omitted in the original plans, and by then it should have been apparent that no one was interested in the canal; so why build them? Col McKerlie was in an unenviable position, especially as his evidence made little impression on the committee.

Its report appeared in 1878 and there were some harsh words about the canal in its pages. Noting that the trustees were 'doubtless very insufficiently aware of the cumbersome charge they were taking over' the report continued:

> The absolutely useless condition of the canal, indeed, was only made clear in the report of Mr Pratt . . . immediately after the transfer had taken place. That report was duly forwarded to the Board of Works; but the facts disclosed in it, which are tolerably conclusive, have never been made public till now . . . The Board made no inquiry into the validity of these allegations, but contented themselves with denying their responsibility and refusing to undertake the repairs. There is in consequence no counter official report to show what was at the time the condition of the canal; but if eighteen years ago the works were in the state pointed out by Mr Pratt, and nothing has since been done to improve them, it is no wonder that the canal should now be choked with mud and weeds, and be utterly useless.[21]

Noting that the canal 'to all intents and purposes is closed' the committee regretted that the BOW, which had spent many thousands of pounds since 1865 on the Ulster Canal, had 're-fused to be consenting parties to the smallest expenditure' on the Ballinamore Canal. On the much-discussed wider question of the wisdom of retaining all the 'northern waterways' the committee was unsure and it recommended the setting up of a royal commission to investigate the matter.

In contrast to the trustees and Fermanagh Grand Jury, the Crichton Committee had its wish for a further inquiry granted. In 1881 a royal commission with Viscount Monck as chairman was appointed to investigate the 'System of Navigation which connects Coleraine, Belfast and Limerick', and of course the Ballinamore Canal featured prominently in the evidence which was heard in mid-1881. Once again the redoubtable J. G. V. Porter testified in his picturesque fashion and, although he was no longer officially connected with it, he was highly critical of the condition of the canal. Remarking that it was 'perfectly useless . . . dry land in a great many places', he added that

> You see birds sitting on the mud at some places in the middle of the canal. It is wonderful jobbing. That canal is a chapter in Irish history that ought to be better known.[22]

Robert Manning, BOW engineer, was next to give evidence and he gave details of his 1875 inspection of the western half of the canal. He recounted that all the masonry works were well constructed and in good condition, but that the lock gates were 'completely out of order and gone to decay . . . rotten, in fact'. While he was in the area he had made inquiries and had been told that only eight boats had used the canal. Manning quoted a letter of March 1876 from the trustees in which they expressed their wish to maintain the works for drainage only 'as there is not, and never has been, any traffic of any kind, nor is there likely to be any traffic to justify keeping the navigation part in repair' but, as has been indicated above, by the late 1870s all maintenance was abandoned. An interesting comment from Manning was that he was 'totally against' the combination of drainage and navigation interests. His estimate for the restoration of the whole navigation was some £7,000, but in his opinion the canal should be retained as a drainage artery only.

Were the navigation to be restored there would, even at that early stage, be one very big problem as Manning shrewdly foresaw.

> When I inspected the navigation in 1875, the summit level was not within four feet of the top of the water of the canal; there being no traffic, they did not take any trouble to keep up the top. The consequence of that was that the low skirts about the lakes, especially about Lough Scur, became bare, and naturally the people about tilled that land and improved it, and if you put up the navigation four feet you will flood that land, and it strikes me it will be an extremely difficult matter for the Government or any person else to do it.[23]

This opinion was corroborated by his assistant, Thomas Crosthwaite, who also catalogued some of the defects of the waterway. On the other hand, Pratt in his evidence contended that 'the present state of the canal is against the drainage' and that damage to banks, for example, would be reduced if the weirs were maintained and the proper water level kept up. Possibly so, but to restore that level would undoubtedly cause flooding problems. Pratt was of the opinion that a trade could be built up on the canal, on the basis of his solitary trial trip, but as the trustees had no power to operate boats there was little chance of this happening. However, he did not think the trustees, even if authorised, should raise money by a levy on an area which he felt was too small and would thus be overburdened.

The report of the Commission, issued in 1882, outlined the history of the canal right from the start and gave details of its condition. It agreed with those who dismissed its utility as a navigable waterway.

> The evidence submitted to us goes to show that the restoration of the navigation would be of little benefit to the public, that there would be no profitable traffic upon it, and further that there would be a great disinclination on the part of the local taxpayers to support it.
>
> The canal has, however, a completely different aspect when viewed as a drainage work. The evidence is unanimous that for drainage purposes it is most valuable, and that it is of great importance that it should be maintained as an arterial drain.
>
> We recommend that no attempt be made at present to re-establish navigation with public money, and we are of the opinion that the canal should be handed over to trustees, to be preserved and improved as a drainage work only, with this obligation, however, that the banks of the canal, and the masonry of the locks shall be maintained in good repair, so that navigation may be resumed at some future time without incurring any very serious expense, if the circumstances of the country shall require it, the Commissioners of Public Works being empowered to execute the necessary works at the expense of the locality on default by the trustees.[24]

A lone member of the commission dissented from the report, holding that the canal 'never had a fair trial', but his voice went unheard. Indeed, there was no detectable reaction to the report either, and it was quickly forgotten. No changes were made in the *status quo*, which in practice meant that the canal was allowed to continue its deterioration without interruption from maintenance or repair activity of any kind.

# CHAPTER 6

# A Partial Revival (1880–1935)

It is a farce calling it navigation. Still, things have to be done.

*S. B. Roe, trustee, 1906*

THE position regarding the navigation in the 1880s is very obscure indeed. No meetings are known to have been held by the trustees between 1878 and 1893, yet there must have been some trustees who took a minimal interest in affairs. J. B. Pratt died on 1 February 1886 and soon afterwards John Joseph Benison took over as acting secretary. But this was largely a nominal post and he did not make any attempt in the 1880s to collect any of the long overdue rents from the spoil bank tenants. No salaries were paid as most of the lock keepers had been 'written off' years before. Presumably they continued to occupy their tiny houses until decay made them uninhabitable. Certainly the houses at Killarcan, Castlefore and Ballinamore continued in occupation until well into this century. The houses at Aghoo, Skelan and Lisconor became empty in time and before long were virtually demolished by people seeking building materials. At Caroul, where there was need for a sluice keeper, Charles Mohan was in residence till his death in the early 1880s; he was succeeded by his sister Mary who remained on the payroll till 1883 and who remained in the house until sometime around the turn of the century.[1] In 1905 the trustees made an unsuccessful attempt to sell the Caroul house and it afterwards went the way of most others. Ballyconnell, with its mills, also needed someone to regulate the levels and the house there remained occupied for the best part of a century.

Because of the necessity to maintain a level for the mills it was essential that both the works at the weir and the upper gates at Ballyconnell lock be kept in repair. Thus in 1880 the latter were the only lock gates in order along the whole canal. Soon afterwards they began to deteriorate and by the middle of the decade they were sorely in need of repair. Under the prescribed procedure a memorial was sent to the BOW which sent Crosthwaite down to investigate. He proposed that a dam be built across the upper end of the lock to keep up the water and a contract was awarded in March 1886 to the miller, William Lang. The work was completed later that year at a cost of £54 which was levied off the surrounding district at the 1887 spring assizes.[2]

The BOW was also involved in another question concerning the Ballyconnell region in 1886. This was the time of the building of the Cavan & Leitrim Railway from Dromod via Ballinamore to Belturbet and Arigna. The BOW was in correspondence with R. A. Macrory, the C & L solicitor, about the height of the bridges by which the Dromod–Belturbet line would cross the canal twice—near Aghoo and just south of Ballyconnell. The latter bridge in particular would obstruct boats by its low headroom and the C & L was queried about it. However, the BOW later washed its hands of the affair:

The Company can act in any way they please, fully accepting all the risk of expense and inconvenience to their traffic if at any time compelled at the instance of those interested in the navigation to raise the bridge over the Woodford River [at Ballyconnell] to the height laid down by the Board.[3]

The C & L took the chance that it would not have to raise the bridge and in the event it was proved correct.

By early 1893 the dam and weir at Ballyconnell needed further attention and again a contract for repairs was awarded to William Lang. Apparently the dam needed reconstruction, while there was a leakage at the weir, and the work cost a total of £125, some £20 more than the contract price. The amount was later levied off the district in the usual fashion and the occasion was notable in that it was the last on which the formal procedure from memorial through to ultimate levy on the ratepayers of any drainage district was put into practice according to the drainage Acts.[4] True, it was nearly being applied again around 1900, also for repairs for the mill level at Ballyconnell, but by then the trustees were back in action and BOW intervention was unnecessary.

For reasons which are now unknown the decision to revive the trustees was taken sometime in 1893. Who took the initiative is also a mystery; it may have been either the grand juries or some of the landowners, both of whom would have been concerned with problems of flooding which would certainly become more serious as the canal channel got ever more choked with silt and decaying vegetation. At any rate, Benison was in contact with Fermanagh Grand Jury early in 1894 and some time later an approach was made to the Roscommon jury, both with a view to having new trustees appointed. The moves suggest that it was interested parties in Cavan and Leitrim who started things moving. Appointment of a permanent secretary was made in 1894 and next year an engineer was chosen. The latter, however, received a token salary payment retrospective to 1886 and it thus appears possible that he had previously been giving advice to Benison and whatever trustees were still interested. By the time a full board of trustees had been appointed (except of course for Roscommon representatives) it was well into 1895 and the first known regular meeting took place on 28 August.

Maintenance works were not undertaken immediately but a necessary preliminary step was soon made—a levy demand was sent to the counties, three of which paid up promptly. The exception was Roscommon and the trustees had to take proceedings against the grand jury to enforce payment. The matter was not resolved until mid-1898 when a judicial decision given in Dublin ordered that payment be made. By 1899 the trustees were ready to recommence maintenance work and once again the location was Ballyconnell, where the weir sluice needed replacement as, possibly, did the dam at the lock. The work was undertaken in mid-year and cost over £120. Evidently there was some local doubt as to the trustees' intentions or abilities and the matter went to the BOW which made an inspection and reported that matters were well in hand.

Progress in general was reasonably good and the trustees could feel quite pleased with it, especially after so long a period of idleness. Possibly the only cloud on the horizon was the lack of enthusiasm on the part of the county authorities (now county councils) when it came to paying the maintenance levies. At this period trustees' meetings were becoming more regular. They were first held in Dublin, as in the old days, and later in Enniskillen, a point which could well indicate the lack of active Leitrim trustees. The first meeting known to have been held in the actual district took place in 1906 at Ballyconnell, which place was the regular venue from 1913 till 1924. Things were still not back to 'normal', however, and some years would elapse before the navigation board settled down to a routine programme which was to go on, albeit with occasional interruptions, for nearly 25 years. No maintenance works were carried out between 1900 and 1907, when repairs were made to the Killarcan house.

This new phase in the life of the canal was also distinguished by its engaging the attention of two more august bodies of inquiry. In 1905 a vice-regal commission on arterial drainage in Ireland was appointed, with Sir Alexander Binnie as chairman, and it heard some evidence on the canal in 1906. One of the trustees, S. B. Roe, gave evidence which confirmed that the trustees were then concentrating mainly on keeping the Ballyconnell works in repair.

The whole expense is keeping up a weir close to the place where I live, which we are bound to keep up for the sake of the mill, small expenses for engineering, and £15 a year which is paid to our secretary.[5]

He also commented on the difficulty in getting payment of the levies, though he stated that Leitrim, not Roscommon, was the culprit.

> We were unfortunately let in for a good deal of law expenses by the County Council of Leitrim. They refused to pay their portion of the assessment, and we had to go to law with them. That ran away with some money, which we in Cavan and the other counties had to pay.[6]

Roe was not exaggerating—in the years previous an inordinate proportion of the total revenue had gone in legal expenses.

Another witness discussed the clash between drainage and navigation interests—the latter needed the water raised to give an adequate depth for boats while for effective drainage the level should be as low as possible. The commission next heard from the Cavan county surveyor, R. N. Somerville, who had some pithy observations to make about 'this great place, Ballyconnell, where they have spent so much money', its mill, and especially the dam built to keep up the water for it and which along with the weir was responsible for flooding.

> They should have bought up this mill and swept it away. If the mill could be bought up the county council in twenty-four hours would buy it up without any loan from the Government, if they had power to do so, and buy up several others as well ... You cannot lower the water one inch on account of an old mill which is worth £24 or £25 a year.[7]

All this was interesting enough, but the canal received far greater attention at the 1906 Royal Commission on Canals and Waterways, which had Baron Shuttleworth as its chairman. This time the report and some appended documents were of greater interest, although some of the evidence was worthy of note. Two witnesses thought that the canal would be a great benefit if restored, while another, Sir Horace Plunkett, although admitting that the drainage consideration was paramount, felt that the navigation could be restored at small relative cost.

*Page 103*   Bridges—2: (*top*) Lisnatullagh bridge; (*centre*) the iron bridge at Drumany; (*bottom*) the new bridge at Carrickmakeegan

*Page 104*    Ballyconnell sluices: (*left*) the sluice at the weir; (*right*) the lock sluice
with the lock house in the background

Rather more negative evidence came from Henry Plews, the general manager of the Great Northern Railway, who stated incorrectly that the BOW had agreed to the building of the low railway bridges by the C & L in 1886–7. While the BOW might indeed have agreed that 'there was no prospect whatever of this canal ever being used for traffic purposes' it had been very careful to point out that the C & L might have to raise its bridges. Plews stated that two bridges would have to be altered and Ballyconnell station moved to a new location were the canal to reopen. One rather gets the impression that it was for other reasons that he painted such a black picture. Possibly he wanted to ensure that there could not be the slightest competition with his own GNR, but it is equally likely that he was holding a watching brief on behalf of the none too prosperous C & L which could ill-afford the alterations which would undoubtedly be necessary in the event of a restoration. But Plews was without doubt correct on one point. To revive the canal would surely involve the ratepayers of the district in additional taxation. And it would surely be untenable for the people to pay towards a canal running in competition with the C & L, for which many of those same ratepayers were already contributing heavily.[8]

One of the members of the commission, R. C. H. Davison, had made a study of the whole Limerick–Belfast waterway network and his findings were appended to the report. He had only a paper knowledge of the Ballinamore Canal, supplemented by what he had heard, but he estimated £49,840 as the cost of restoring the canal to a 6ft depth. Of this amount £10,240 was for lock gates, £30,000 for dredging, £1,600 for masonry repairs, and the rest for raising the C & L bridges and altering the site of Ballyconnell station.[9] Another appendix to the commission report was far more informative. It comprised a report made on 31 January 1906 to the Department of Agriculture and Technical Instruction for Ireland by its engineer, Charles D. Oliver. He had inspected the canal and had called at every lock, although he had not traversed any of it by boat.

In Oliver's opinion the repair of the Leitrim–Lough Scur

G

canal section would cost a trivial amount. The position was different, however, east of the summit level where

> the disappearance of the lock gates, having greatly reduced the level above the weirs, has unduly reduced the section and increased the fall and consequently the velocity, with destructive effect, in addition to allowing a terrific rush of water to pass through a channel (the lock chamber) never designed for the purpose.[10]

To prevent the 'speedy total destruction of the works' he regarded it essential that the upper gates be replaced in the eight locks on this sector or, if navigation was to be abandoned, a concrete barrier might be substituted at each lock. He rightly stated that only a fully detailed survey would reveal the extent and the cost of repairs necessary if the navigation were to be restored, but he noted that from his observations there seemed to be no insuperable difficulties and he thought that £6,000 would be 'a liberal guess'. He suggested that £1,250 should be urgently spent for drainage purposes and that a further £2,500 might permit a reopening of the navigation from Lough Erne to Ballinamore, or £4,500 for the whole length.

He was definite, however, that 'any such further outlay should only be contemplated in the event of some definite proposal, adequately guaranteed, for the working of the navigation being brought forward' for when the canal was in working condition no boats used it. He added the opinion that he strongly doubted that any restoration schemes would 'fail to meet with opposition from counties taxed for the maintenance of a railway parallel'. Oliver's general report was supplemented by a detailed report which revealed very well the state of many features of the canal some 50 years after their construction.

The report of the commission sketched out as usual the history of the canal and commented on its management.

> The works were, in 1860, by a device singularly calculated to promote inefficient management, transferred to two bodies of trustees, one for drainage purposes, both bodies having powers of taxation for maintenance purposes.[11]

The members of the commission felt that not enough evidence
had been submitted to justify them in recommending the restoration of the canal, but they added—as did both the Crichton
and Monck inquiries—the opinion that

> this canal should be maintained as a drain, and the masonry and
> other works kept in good repair, so that it could be readily con-
> verted into a navigable waterway if the time should come when
> it becomes desirable to connect the River Shannon with the
> Northern Canal System and the port of Belfast.[12]

It had all been said before and the reaction was exactly the
same this time. No change took place; the trustees remained in
control and they continued to ignore the navigational features,
instead trying to achieve as efficient a drainage as was possible
with their limited efforts. Their attempts were not exactly
appreciated locally, if Fermanagh County Council was anything to go by.

> Choked up in parts with weeds, and actually dry in other parts,
> it is a monument of wasted capital and a striking evidence of
> the futility of trustee control.[13]

Ballyconnell was becoming a trouble spot again by about
1905. The lock dam was still extant, but there was trouble at
the weir where the large overflow sluice was out of action,
causing flooding at times of heavy flow. The trustees called on
Somerville in 1907 to prepare plans and an estimate for the
work which was advertised in September. The work included
the repair or reconstruction of a bridge across the headrace beside the mill, and when there was no response to the advertisements trustee S. B. Roe had this presumably urgent part of the
work done. The main work at the weir was readvertised in 1908
and 1909, also without success, and it was not until 1911 that
the sluice was repaired, then apparently by direct labour under
the direction of Irwin, the engineer to the trustees. The effort
seems to have exhausted the energies of the trustees who did
little for the next two years.

But this was, in fact, quite an important transition period.

Under the Local Government Act of 1898 the old grand juries were replaced by county councils as from mid-1899.[14] All the rights and obligations concerning navigations passed to the councils but the change was none the less very significant. The grand jurors were for the most part prominent landowners who (however well-disposed they were) were remote from the troubles which stemmed from the canal. True, they owned the lands which suffered periodic damage from flooding and they bore some of the financial burden, but it was their tenants who lost their crops or had to make lengthy detours to the markets when bridges collapsed. The trustees they appointed were of the same caste; indeed the qualification laid down by the 1856 Act ensured this. Thus the navigation board at any time up to around 1910 would have consisted of some inactive members, some who were enthusiastic—notably J. G. V. Porter in his day —and some with no more than a passing interest in the duties involved. The net effect was that the board was decidedly on the lethargic side. Now under the new arrangement the county councils, composed of democratically-elected members, would be sure to include some of the community directly suffering from the vagaries of the canal. In turn, council-appointed trustees could be expected to take a livelier interest in the problems caused by the navigation.

However, the county councils did not make a clean break and suddenly replace 'grand jury trustees' with men of their own choosing. Rather, there was a transition period of some 20 years during which the older men died or resigned from the board and were replaced by council appointees. The years 1912-13 were a landmark in that a third of the board was replaced by new men; the new blood would prove very beneficial. A step of equal importance was the election by the trustees of a new chairman, Francis McGovern. He had joined the board some years earlier, possibly around 1906, and his becoming chairman was to ensure that as much benefit as possible would be reaped from as much maintenance work as the pitiful resources of the board would allow. The next quarter-century was to prove the busiest period in the history of the navigation since the award and the one pity was that the effort was directed solely towards drainage, all thoughts of navigation having been abandoned. Had McGovern been in control in the vital years after 1860 perhaps the story would have been very different.

A significant feature of the new era was the holding of regular board meetings. The trustees met on average three times a year, normally in January, April and July. At their first meeting they would consider the estimates for the half-year just beginning and study the maintenance programme proposed by the engineer. In April they would award contracts for the various works and in July the business would again be largely financial. The different contractors would have to be paid and there would be the task of drawing up the estimates and making a levy demand for the second half-year. Rather, would the trustees approve or amend the estimates which the secretary had prepared for the board. There never was a treasurer, so all money matters fell to the secretary.[15]

The normal procedure in preparing the estimates was simple enough. The engineer submitted to the secretary an estimate of the amount which he thought would be needed for the maintenance works planned for the period in question. To this sum the latter added appropriate amounts to cover salaries and other probable expenditure, but he deducted from the total any sums to the credit of the trustees and also the probable income from rents. The net amount left would then be carefully apportioned among the four counties precisely as laid down by the navigation award. The financial statement, along with a full account of expenditure during the past half-year, was then sent to the counties, whose duty it was to meet the levy.

The secretary was responsible for the collection of rent from the tenants. The average yearly rental was small but, despite the effort involved in collecting it, it was useful in helping to keep down the levy demands. One of the problems facing the revived board in the 1890s was the restoration of this income to its former level. As it turned out, however, this proved impossible as too long had elapsed since the last rent demand had been made, and when the board tried legal action against some Leitrim tenants around 1900 the statute of limitations was invoked. A second reason for the very uneven distribution of paying tenants was that the lands available for letting by the trustees were those which had been purchased for the canal in the 1850s, and these would not have included all, if any, of the original river banks.

In the selection of the maintenance works to be carried out the trustees were guided by their engineer, whose recommendations in turn were based both on requests from farmers for specific improvements and on his own observations made on inspection. The engineer, or superintendent as he was more usually known, would also draw up plans, specifications and estimates for the works which would on approval be advertised and let on contract. This policy was by and large very successful, though at times the going was rough enough for the navigation board. Over the years it received a multitude of complaints from aggrieved people along the canal who often suffered severe losses and who were driven to seek the aid of a solicitor. But there was no long history of legal action and the trustees were just about able to keep the situation under control. This was no mean achievement, considering that the average of the 26 half-yearly total levy demands made in the period 1913–35 was just under £125.

Maintenance work began in earnest in 1913 and it was appropriate that the first work to be carried out was on the channel itself rather than on some of the works. It had been nearly 40 years since such a work had been undertaken and it was not before time when William Coulston was given the task of cutting and removing 'trees, shrubs, bushes and brambles' between Ballyconnell and Caroul locks. In 1914 attention was turned to the stretch just west of Garadice Lake and another important work was carried out at Ballyconnell. It was the trustees' intention that their work should be directed towards flood abatement, hence the clearing of the channel, and it was obvious that something would have to be done at Ballyconnell where the weir and its sluice (even when the latter was in working order) were not fully capable of handling heavy flood-water discharges.

The dam across the face of the lock did not help matters in the least and it was agreed early in 1914 that it should be re-placed by a large sluice where the upper gates of the lock once were. The supply of the sluice, to the engineer's specifications, was put out to tender and a contract was soon awarded to A. & J. Main & Co of Dublin. The board had to spend further to have the large steel sluice put into place and, ironically, it had to pay also to have the weir repaired to conserve water in times of low flow. It was indeed a ludicrous situation—at the one time the trustees had in hands works designed for opposing pur-poses.

In the years following, Ballyconnell continued to occupy an excessive amount of the trustees' time. The new sluice needed attention in 1916 and 1917. By 1919 the sluice gates at the weir were very rotten and had to be replaced, the work being done by direct labour. Despite this the mill was idle in 1920 because of a leakage at both lock and weir sluices, and around this time local resentment at the periodic flooding which could still be caused by the set-up at Ballyconnell crystallised into action when the weir sluice was maliciously damaged. And, another irony, the forcible removal of the obstruction at Ballyconnell, while relieving flooding back towards Skelan, caused a greater flow down towards Caroul where the channel was blocked with debris and the net result was flooding around Cloncoohy instead. The damage was repaired temporarily, possibly by the miller, apparently not by the trustees for the board had been reduced in numbers by deaths and, shortly, the state of the country in general would not be such that normal activities could be carried on.

The meeting of July 1922 was to be the last for 18 months—the Civil War was occupying people's attention. The political scene had quietened down sufficiently by the beginning of 1924 to permit the trustees to resume their activities. Three new men to represent Leitrim were appointed by Commissioner P. Sugrue, who was acting in place of the county council which had been suspended. The presence of the new Leitrim representatives led to a change in the procedure for meetings. Since Francis McGovern had become chairman all had been held in Ballyconnell but now a system of holding meetings alternately at the courthouses in Ballyconnell and Ballinamore was introduced; it was adhered to almost without interruption throughout the active period of the board.

The topic of maintenance was on the agenda for the January 1924 meeting and a deputation from Fermanagh attended to describe the flooding caused by obstructions at Caroul lock. Many farmers were thinking of taking legal action, so bad was the position. The trustees were agreed that the work was necessary but they decided not to undertake it until recent levy arrears had been paid by Fermanagh County Council. To spend money levied off the other counties on works in Fermanagh would, it was felt, be unfair. That was the general policy adopted by the trustees. As far as was practical money levied off a county was spent on maintenance in that county. This was all very well but the unfortunate Roscommon ratepayers were thus left with a levy which went towards the administrative costs of works which were of no concern to them.

For ratepayers of the other three counties, however, the works were decidedly useful, especially as many of the contracts now being awarded were for work on the actual channel. Any cleaning work carried out on it was bound to have a beneficial effect on the neighbouring lands, and it also rendered more effective the work of the drainage trustees, who regularly had the lateral drains under their control cleaned. From time to time the scope of the navigation maintenance would be widened to include the replacement or reconstruction of accommodation bridges in need of attention.[16]

It was inevitable, of course, that Ballyconnell should appear

# BALLINAMORE & BALLYCONNELL NAVIGATION DISTRICT.

# NOTICE TO CONTRACTORS

The Trustees for the Ballinamore and Ballyconnell Navigation District, will, at their Meeting to be held in the Courthouse, Ballinamore, on Saturday, 22nd day of April, 1933, be prepared to receive and consider Tenders for the following works :--

## COUNTY CAVAN

**No. 1.** Removing Sand Bank out of bed of Canal at rere of Mrs. Clancy's premises in Ballyconnell. Cost not to exceed £5.

**No. 2.** Removing Bank out of Canal at Weir Wall, Ballyconnell. Cost not to exceed £5.

## COUNTY FERMANAGH

**No. 3.** Removing Slips out of Canal, in the townland of Cloncooley. Cost not to exceed £5.

## COUNTY LEITRIM

**No. 4.** To clean 300 perches of Canal, in sections, from Lough Scur to Bridge on County road at Kilclare. Cost not to exceed £50.

The works to be carried out in strict accordance with the specifications prepared by Mr. EDWARDS, C.E., Superintendent, and in time to be fixed by the Trustees for completing the Contracts.

The lowest or any Tender not necessarily accepted.

**By Order,**

**PETER EDWARDS, C.E.**

Bawnboy, 31st March, 1933. **JOHN PRIOR, Secretary**

ANGLO-CELT, LTD., PRINTING WORKS, CAVAN

FIG 9. A typical latter-day notice to contractors, 1933

in the maintenance programme once more. In 1929 there were complaints about both sluices, especially that at the weir which had been replaced by a wooden obstruction of planks after it had been damaged in 1920. This latter obstruction was causing drainage problems as far back as the west side of Garadice Lake, and the trouble was not solved by a decision to have the planks removed in time of flood. The trustees met the complaint to some extent by having the leakage at the lock sluice repaired.

But this action did nothing to relieve the plight of the farmers who began to think more and more of legal action. Things came to a head in mid-1931 when there was such heavy rain that the people in Boeshill, near Garadice, lost their entire hay crop; in places boats had to be used to rescue cattle. Boeshill was not the only townland affected; farmers in Cormeen, Tubberlion, Coologe, Skelan, Ballyheady, Lecharrownahone and elsewhere were very irate indeed over the lack of a sluice at the weir and they made their grievance clearly known. With commendable speed it was agreed to have a new sluice erected, and the work was shortly afterwards put in hand. This was the last effort put in by the trustees on the Ballyconnell sluices which had occupied so much time and work. The work was rounded off in 1932 and 1933 when sand banks were removed from the channel near the weir and some repairs were carried out to the fish pass.

The trustees had certainly given Ballyconnell and its problems all the attention they could and it made a refreshing change when, in the mid-1930s, they concerned themselves with Ballinamore. The basin there was in a highly insanitary condition because of sewage discharges and in times of low flow the position was acute. The trustees were asked to deal with the problem and although arguably not their concern they awarded contracts for cleaning work in 1933 and later years. The last such contract was given in September 1935, for the cleaning of the channel from lock No 5 to the basin and of the old river course for a short distance to Stradermot, a total length of about 250 statute perches. The work was duly executed and what distinguishes it is that, although nobody knew it at the time, it was the last maintenance contract of any kind awarded by the trustees of the navigation district.

CHAPTER 7

# The Final Decline?
# (1936–71)

> If the Americans can cross the world to play ping-
> pong with the Chinese after Korea, the Irish have not
> alone an opportunity but a duty to show themselves
> mature enough to establish this bridge over troubled
> waters.
>
> Irish Press *Editorial on the*
> *proposed Shannon–Erne link, 1971*

APART from a short period in the middle of the last century
when the grand juries were seduced by rosy prospects into
agreeing to bear financial responsibility for the canal in future
years, the county authorities always viewed the navigation with
disfavour, which manifested itself as early as the 1860s. By the
1930s this dissatisfaction reached a peak and the counties were
coming to the conclusion that the question should be settled
once and for all. The region 'served' by the canal was essentially
a depressed area and its local authorities were always seeking to
obtain the best value possible for the money they levied in
rates. In their view there was little if any worth while return to
be gained from contributing towards the piecemeal and inadequate maintenance of a white elephant of a navigation.

Leitrim County Council, which had 'always resisted the rate'[1]
for the upkeep of the canal, took decisive action in 1936 and
instituted legal proceedings against the trustees on a number of
grounds. It claimed that there was doubt over the trustees'
qualifications, that is, whether or not they had the land holdings

specified by the 1856 Act to be held by any trustee,[2] and also that for the navigation board to be properly constituted representatives of all counties should be present. Perhaps more important was the claim that the provisions of the 1856 Act affecting the councils in the 26-Counties were 'inconsistent with the constitution and inoperative'.[3] The council terminated the appointments of its trustees by resolution in 1936[4] and in the following year the remaining trustees, representing Cavan and Fermanagh, resigned shortly after the last board meeting to be held for a long time. For over three years nothing apparently happened. The court action had not yet come to a hearing and of course no maintenance work was being carried out. There was an unexpected development in 1940 when Fermanagh County Council appointed three new trustees, the only nominal trustees in office for some years.[5]

At a preliminary hearing early in 1942 the Attorney-General was added to the list of defendants and a few months later the action was heard in the High Court, Dublin, before Mr Justice Black. The hearing took six days between 30 June and 10 July and there was much deep legal argument, concentrating mainly on the question of whether or not the presence of trustees appointed by a 6-County authority led to a situation inconsistent with the 26-County constitution.[6] The action was described by one of the counsel participating as 'one of not very great importance from the point of view of the ratepayers of the counties involved, but one that could amount to something in the political and administrative sense'.[7] The issues were complex enough to result in judgement being reserved and it was not for a year that the decision was given. The judge gave his opinion on 30 July 1943—the case was dismissed on all counts, nothing being found unconstitutional about the situation.[8] Possibly on that account the judge had been impressed by examples of other bodies on which 'foreign representatives' sat —notably the Great Northern Railway and the Representative Church Body—which had been cited by counsel.[9]

The decision left the three new Fermanagh trustees as the

sole persons in charge of the navigation district. One wonders what was their reaction to being in control of a navigation which for by far the greater part of its length lay outside the 6-Counties. Enniskillen, appropriately, was the venue for the first meeting of this new navigation board, held on 4 July 1944. After over 8 years' inactivity one would have expected that there would have been a backlog of complaints arising from the non-maintenance of the channel. This does not seem to have been the case, although there had been serious trouble due to flooding in the Drumlonan area near Carrickmakeegan in autumn 1943.

To investigate the position fully the trustees decided to have a full survey made of the canal. Peter Edwards, the engineer to the board, had died early in 1937 and so it was decided to advertise the commission. Following an advertisement in a national newspaper in October 1944 the duty of making the survey was entrusted to Patrick Gaffney, an engineer from Cavan. Little time was lost and after arrangements had been made in December, Mr Gaffney, accompanied by Patrick Quinn, the secretary to the trustees, carried out his survey in January. He spent five days on the job and with his companion examined the whole canal, walking most of the way but taking a boat from Garadice to Skelan. The report on the canal was completed in time for the March 1945 board meeting, but it was hardly to be considered, let alone implemented, for there was a problem in the form of a continuing absence of funds.[10] The result was another hiatus pending some action by the councils in the 26-Counties. Meanwhile problems were arising along the canal, principally with the accommodation bridges. That at Lisnatullagh was by 1945 in such a state that it could not be used. On the last occasion it was used a mare had fallen through it. People along the canal were tired of complaining; they were now seeking compensation for damage and loss.[11]

For over two years more there were no significant developments until, in May 1947, both the Leitrim and Cavan councils appointed three new trustees each. While this may have seemed a promising move there was no follow-up in the form of funds, and the position was not hopeful when the board met on 6 February 1948. This time decisive action, in a sense, came from the trustees. Deciding that there was little point in maintaining an anomalous situation, they ceased their activities, though these now consisted merely of meeting irregularly. This was the last meeting in the 91-year life of the Ballinamore and Bally-connell Navigation Trustees and once the trustees left Bally-connell on that February afternoon the canal went into a state of suspended animation, or rather, it continued to decay quietly as it had done for so long previously. Shortly after the trustees ceased to function, the bridge over the canal at Derry-macoffin collapsed—the event was something of a symbolic occurrence.

However, the county councils were aware of the problems which the canal could cause and from 1948 onwards they under-took some important work which might well have been beyond the capabilities of the trustees. They repaired the accommoda-tion bridges as necessary. Soon after the old bridge collapsed a concrete span was placed across the channel at Derrymacoffin, and at Cloncoohy a similar structure was erected in place of the rather infamous old bridge. The bridge at Carrickmakeegan, built as an accommodation bridge but which had long carried a public road, collapsed late in 1968 as a lorry laden with sand was crossing it. After a reconstruction period during which the bridge at Derrygoan was the nearest substitute, the new bridge was opened in 1971. It is a lofty concrete structure with massive, elaborately fenced and banked approaches and its height is such that no one can accuse Leitrim County Council of failing to provide sufficient headroom for any future boats.

After the previous decade the 1950s were very quiet. The canal became a more or less accepted nuisance, though still one which could cause great hardship. There was periodic talk of great new drainage schemes for the region; as early as 1950 a government representative addressed Leitrim County Council, promising a comprehensive scheme and intimating that once the work had been completed a new controlling authority would be established, consisting of representatives of Cavan and Leitrim only. Later on the BOW under a relief scheme carried out some clearing work along the canal.

A decade later the periodic flooding had become such a nuisance that a meeting was held in Templeport Hall to discuss the matter but there were no positive results. A reading of the local newspapers reveals just how serious the flooding could be. One weekend's rain could mean a rise in water level of three feet if not more and on occasion overflow of the banks has been the consequence.[12] Besides directly flooding land itself the canal caused, and indeed still causes, problems with the lateral drains maintained annually by the drainage trustees. When the level in the main channel is high the water backs up in these drains and quite often very large tracts of land are inundated. Around Ballinamore the trouble is most serious at Drumraine, where the road can be made impassable, and at Carrick-makeegan. Very often the worst trouble is caused by sudden summer floods during which large discharges rush into the overgrown channel which cannot cope with the flow. On 15 August 1970, for example, there were severe losses by farmers; one, who saw ten of his hay-cocks swept away, commented that a further half-day's rain would have meant the loss of his entire crop. It is thus perfectly understandable that the riparian farmers, especially in the region between Ballinamore and Garadice, have a somewhat jaundiced view of the canal and are not in the least enthusiastic about its possible restoration.

Their views are not shared, however, by the protagonists of the canal, among whom has been for some years past Leitrim County Council. The council, keeping an eye on the increasing number of pleasure boats on the Shannon and, indeed, fostering the growth by undertaking an excellent development of facilities at Carrick-on-Shannon, had come round to the opinion that a combined drainage and navigation scheme should be carried out and had approached the Department of

Transport and Power on the subject. The latter had been reported as quoting the BOW view that

> the design of a scheme for the restoration of the navigation in
> conjunction with the improvement of the drainage would re-
> quire a lot of study and design work, and they added that it will
> be some years yet before the question of this canal can be taken
> up under the Arterial Drainage Act, 1945.[13]

Another demand for action came in 1969 when the Inland
Waterways Association of Ireland, which had established
branches at both Ballinamore and Ballyconnell, called for a
survey by a competent firm, being supported by the council. In
1970 Leitrim County Council again pressed for a survey by the
BOW, which had dismayed some councillors by pointing out
that the Erne catchment was the tenth on the priority list of the
arterial drainage programme and also that

> the Erne as a whole was a very large catchment and presented
> engineering problems of great complexity. It was furthermore
> complicated by the problem of the Border, and consequently a
> complete scheme would take a very long time to develop as far
> as the work stage.[14]

The arguments did not impress the council one little bit, the
county engineer commenting that the BOW engineers were
well capable of putting forward proposals for drainage and
navigation which did not conflict. And as for the border question, there would surely be no difficulty on that account, for
previously representatives of the Northern Ireland tourist
board had indicated a willingness to co-operate in and share the
cost of a survey of the canal. What further annoyed the councillors was the fact that a survey had been made of another of
the Erne sub-catchments, the Finn, which also runs through
Northern Ireland in places, yet it was claimed that such a survey
would not be feasible at present on the Ballinamore Canal/
Woodford catchment. The general displeasure was succinctly
expressed by one speaker

> Tourism and agriculture are the only apparent solution to de-
> velopment in County Leitrim and we should expect that a

H

Government Department like the Office of Public Works would be pressing forward such a scheme rather than deferring it.[15]

The canal was by then fairly well in the public eye. For a few years past international student work-camps had been set up in summer along the canal and much cleaning work had been carried out. In addition, enthusiasts had dredged the basin at Ballinamore. The IWAI had published some articles and notes relating to the canal and advocating its reopening, and in 1969 its local branches had held their first boat rally during which a flotilla of small boats had gone from Ballinamore to Ballyconnell. The canal also played a part in the programme of events for the Ballinamore town festivals in 1969 and 1970. Short boat rides were given along the stretch from Ballinamore basin to Lock 5 at Ardrum. A level had been obtained by placing a barrier of sleepers across the masonry works at Ardrum. This action, however, gave local farmers a foretaste of what the restoration of the canal might well bring for, after a very rainy night, the barrier caused the water to back up in a number of drains and streams running into the canal; those affected were not amused.

The pro-canal publicity continued into 1971 with occasional letters to the press advocating the restoration as a means of promoting north/south co-operation. One of a series of articles on Irish waterways in the *Irish Times* called attention to the potential of the canal, drawing a small correspondence in return.[16] But all this was nothing compared to the lead story in the *Irish Press* of 20 May 1971 which proclaimed that

> A link-up between the Rivers Erne and Shannon will be one of the first specific projects to be considered in the new North-South talks on economic co-operation.

The report stated that the Minister for Transport and Power in the Republic had put forward the proposal which was warmly endorsed in the lead editorial. Tourist officials were understandably enthusiastic about the idea. Questions were asked in parliament a little later on, when it began to emerge that there would be no speedy reopening of the whole canal but rather a more modest start with the restoration of the section from Ballyconnell to the Erne, which would give a waterway link to Belturbet. The minister stated that an interim survey was being carried out on the stretch below Ballyconnell. That was on 27 May, at which time a team was actually in the field taking levels and surveying at Caroul lock, one of the two which would have to be restored.

On the question of a reopening west of Ballyconnell the minister was less specific, noting that 'the drainage of the Woodford Canal, between Ballyconnell, Co Cavan, and Ballinamore, Co Leitrim, was a long-term proposal'.[17] This would be an extension which would depend on a detailed survey. The impression was conveyed that the reopening of the whole canal, however desirable, would not be a step too quickly taken, on the grounds of engineering complexity and overall cost. Not that the former reason would seem to count for much if one took account of an enthusiastic article on 'the forgotten canal' with which the *Irish Press* followed up its original story.[18]

The reality, however, would be rather different. Much work would have to be done to make the waterway navigable for any reasonable size of boat. While the masonry bridges are in fine condition this is not so of some of the locks. Those west of Lough Scur are in good order but those on the river navigation, notably that at Ballinamore, would all require greater or lesser attention. Weirs, too, are in places in bad condition and would need much restoration. The fish passes and recesses for the overflow sluices are almost everywhere a problem, and there would be headroom difficulties with some of the accommodation bridges. But the biggest problems would be caused by the raising of the water level to give a depth of at least 3½ft throughout the canal. Without question much land would be flooded by such a move, which would offend a considerable body of public opinion. However much the people along the canal would like to welcome boating visitors to their district, they largely earn a living from land which is often poor and is rendered worse by the canal when it floods. Because the raising of the water would interfere with the drainage work still being carried out, a very wide area of land would be affected. Without very extensive dredging and clearing there is no alternative to a significant raising of the water level and, if one remembers the difficulty in getting an adequate depth in Lough Scur in 1860, when the canal should have been in its best condition, there seems to be little merit in suggestions that the sills of the locks at either end of the summit level be lowered.

On the other hand, if governmental approval were given for a full scale drainage scheme on the lines of those carried out on the rivers Moy or Inny by the BOW, using modern equipment and techniques, there is no doubt that flood relief could be achieved along with the making of a navigable waterway. What is needed is a thoroughly critical professional survey of the canal and an accurately prepared estimate of the cost of its restoration. The information thus made available should enable all the parties interested in the canal, either as protagonists or antagonists, to come to the best decision.

As a first step it was revealed late in 1971 that a 'visual survey' had shown that at least £100,000 would have to be spent to restore navigation to enable cabin cruisers to travel from Lough Erne 'to at least as far as Ballyconnell'. It was thought that the work would take three summer seasons to complete and that a detailed field survey, made over two months, would be necessary in order to enable firm estimates to be prepared. It had been hoped that such a survey would be arranged soon but the political unrest in the north had made it necessary to defer any investigation.[19]

One can but hope, then, that a full survey setting out the true position along the whole navigation will be made as soon as circumstances permit. Then can the governments consider the matter and, hopefully, give their approval for the reopening of the Ballinamore Canal—an ill-thought of, unhappy navigation in the past, but one which in future would unify two already fine waterway systems, giving Ireland an unsurpassed network of inland navigations.

# Notes

## NOTES TO CHAPTER 1 (*pages 13–21*)

1. V. T. H. & D. R. Delany, *The Canals of the South of Ireland*, 1966, p 98. This is the basic source for general waterway history in the south of Ireland and much use has been made of it in the present chapter.
2. W. A. McCutcheon, *The Canals of the North of Ireland*, 1965, p 99. This is a companion volume to the above and similar use has been made of it.
3. M. B. Mullins, 'An Historical Sketch of Engineering in Ireland', *Trans. Inst. Civil Engineers (Ireland)* (1863), VI, p 148.
4. *Report of William Chapman, Engineer, on the means of making Woodford River navigable from Lough-Erne to Woodford-Lough . . .*, 1793.
5. Chapman, p 9.
6. Ibid.
7. McCutcheon, p 99.

## NOTES TO CHAPTER 2 (*pages 22–35*)

1. 1 & 2 Will IV, c 33, 1831.
2. V. T. H. & D. R. Delany, *The Canals of the South of Ireland*, 1966, p 113ff details the history of the Shannon Navigation.
3. W. T. Mulvany, *Report . . . on a preliminary examination of the country between the Rivers Shannon and Erne with a view to the formation of a Proposed Junction Canal . . .*, 1839.
4. Mulvany, p 5.
5. Ibid, p 13.
6. Ibid.
7. M. B. Mullins, 'An Historical Sketch of Engineering in Ireland', *Trans. Inst. Civil Engineers (Ireland)* (1863), VI.
8. 8 & 9 Vic, c 69.
9. 9 Vic, c 4.
10. 10 & 11 Vic, c 79.

## NOTES TO CHAPTER 3 (*pages 36–56*)

1. McCutcheon, p 98.
2. Parliamentary Papers (PP), *38*, 287 (1852/3), gives the dates of memorials and

other preliminary steps. Most of the detailed information for this chapter has been taken from the BOW MS records in the Public Record Office of Ireland (PROI). A long series of volumes contains a vast amount of correspondence which has been drawn on extensively. To avoid an excessive number of notes only leading references are given. The preliminary stages of the project are covered by volumes with the following PROI reference numbers: I/11/5/1, I/11/5/2 in the 'Drainage Letters' (the most important series) and I/11/2.

3. PROI: I/11/2, 5 August 1844.
4. PROI: I/11/5/2, 10 September 1844.
5. PROI: I/11/5/1, 12 August 1844.
6. PROI: I/11/5/1, 12 August 1844.
7. PROI: I/11/5/2, 2 November 1844.
8. Report of the Commissioners of Inquiry into Arterial Drainage in Ireland upon the Ballinamore and Ballyconnell Drainage and Navigation District . . ., contained in PROI: I/11/4.
9. PROI: I/11/5/2, 28 June 1845.
10. PROI: I/11/4. See note 8.
11. PROI: I/11/6/4, 4 February 1854.
12. PROI: II/11/1/6, July/August 1846.
13. PROI: I/11/1/2, 4 March 1847. PROI: I/11/4. See note 8.
14. PROI: I/11/9/1, 7 August 1847.
15. PROI: I/11/9/1, 30 September 1847.
16. PROI: I/11/9/2, 6 December 1848.
17. Much of the detail in following pages is taken from the Annual Reports of the BOW which contained reports by the engineers in charge of the various districts. The first annual report was issued in 1832.
18. PROI: I/11/9/2, 16 March 1850.
19. PROI: I/11/9/2, 13 March 1850; II/11/3/1.
20. PROI: I/11/4. See note 8.
21. PROI: I/11/9/2, 4 July 1849.
22. 20th Annual Report of BOW.
23. PROI: I/11/9/3, 24 September 1851.
24. PP, *38*, 287 (1852/3).

### NOTES TO CHAPTER 4 (*pages* 57–77)

1. PROI: I/11/6/4, 28 January 1854.
2. PROI: I/11/8/7, 29 October 1853. For this chapter also, the source of most of the detailed information is the series of letter books relating to drainage in the PROI. The volumes of particular relevance have PROI references in the I/11/5 series of general drainage letters.
3. PROI: I/11/6/4, 16 January 1854.
4. 18 & 19 Vic, c 110.
5. PROI: I/11/5/9, 20 November 1854.
6. 23rd Annual Report of BOW. These reports are also heavily drawn on in the present chapter.
7. PROI: I/11/5/8, 15 March 1854.
8. 23rd Annual Report of BOW.
9. PROI: I/11/9/3, 4 February 1853.

10. PROI: I/11/5/9, 27 July 1854
11. Ibid, 1 September & 13 September 1854.
12. PROI: II/11/3/7, September & November 1855. All the financial details of the district appear in the ledgers: II/11/1/1, II/11/1/6, II/11/3/1, 4, 7.
13. PROI: I/11/5/9, 10 October 1854.
14. PROI: I/11/5/16, 26 January 1859.
15. 24th Annual Report of BOW.
16. PROI: I/11/5/12, 29 January 1856; 25th Annual Report of BOW.
17. PROI: I/11/5/9, 29 July 1854.
18. 26th Annual Report of BOW.
19. 19 & 20 Vic, c 62, s 2.
20. Ibid, s 10.
21. PROI: I/11/5/15, 19 July 1858.
22. 27th Annual Report of BOW.
23. Ibid.
24. PROI: I/11/5/17, 17 April 1860.
25. PROI: I/11/4. Inquiry Commissioners' Report, 1859.
26. PROI: I/11/6/4, 20 January & 4 February 1854.
27. PROI: I/11/5/17, 16 March 1860.

## NOTES TO CHAPTER 5 (*pages* 78–97)

1. PROI: I/11/5/17, 9 July 1860, 24 July 1860; I/1/5/6, 24 July 1860.
2. PROI: ibid, 5 December 1860. This volume contains correspondence with the trustees on various matters.
3. PROI: I/11/5/17, 19 June 1861.
4. Information communicated by Mr Walter Levinge. Much of the information contained in following pages (and chapters) has come from personal communications with many people interested in and resident in the area served by the canal.
5. PROI: I/11/5/17, 1 February 1861.
6. PROI: I/1/5/6, 11 July 1861.
7. PROI: I/11/5/17, 20 November 1860.
8. Ibid, 30 January 1861.
9. PP, *23* (1878), minute 2739—Proceedings of Crichton Committee in which Pratt's report is quoted in full.
10. PROI: I/11/5/17, 20 November 1860.
11. PROI: I/1/5/6, 4 April 1860.
12. Ibid.
13. PP, *21* (1882), minute 2168.
14. Ibid, Report, p 15.
15. 44th Annual Report of BOW.
16. PROI: I/11/7/6, 28 May 1875; I/11/7/7, 17 August 1876 & 19 January 1877.
17. PROI: I/11/7/6, 18 June 1875.
18. PP, *23* (1878), minute 2621.
19. Ibid, minute 2629.
20. Ibid, minute 2750.
21. Ibid, Report, p xli.
22. PP, *21* (1882), minute 2167.
23. Ibid, minute 2251.
24. Ibid, Report, p 15.

## NOTES TO CHAPTER 6 (*pages* 98–115)

1. This information and much of that in following paragraphs has come from personal interviews with people resident in the district.
2. PROI: I/1/2/102, 27 March 1886; I/1/2/107, 24 December 1886.
3. PROI: I/1/2/106, 4 October 1886.
4. PROI: II/1/65/12. Contract dated 17 March 1893; evidence of acting chairman, BOW, on 22 January 1923 to Canals and Inland Waterways Commission.
5. PP, Cd 3467 (1907), minute 2777.
6. Ibid, minute 2781.
7. Ibid, minutes 3950, 3953.
8. PP, Cd 3717 (1907), evidence of Plews and others.
9. PP, Cd 5653 (1911), Appendix No 10.
10. Ibid, Appendix No 6.
11. PP, Cd 5626 (1911), p 35, para 136.
12. Ibid, para 319.
13. Ibid, para 138.
14. 61 & 62 Vic, c 37.
15. This general procedure was very similar to that still being operated by the drainage trustees.
16. Details of bridge reconstructions known to have been carried out are given in Appendix 1. There is little available documentation on the navigation district in later years but as most of the contracts awarded were for drainage-oriented works of limited scale this loss is not serious in the present context. Certainly no works of any relevance to navigation were carried out since the early 1870s.

## NOTES TO CHAPTER 7 (*pages* 116–124)

1. *Leitrim Observer* (*LO*), 4 April 1942. See also *LO*, 27 July 1928 for details of earlier resistance to the levy.
2. *LO*, 4 April 1936.
3. *LO*, 4 July 1942.
4. *LO*, 5 September 1936 & 4 July 1942.
5. *LO*, 4 July 1942.
6. *LO*, 4, 11 & 18 July 1942; *Irish Times*, 1, 2, 3, 9 & 11 July 1942.
7. *LO*, 18 July 1942.
8. *Irish Times*, 30 July 1943; *LO*, 27 October 1945.
9. See note 6.
10. *LO*, 27 October 1945.
11. Information in the above and subsequent paragraphs has been obtained from interviews with people living in the district.
12. See, for example, *LO*, 27 December 1969 & 28 February 1970.
13. *LO*, 16 September 1967.
14. *Anglo-Celt*, 12 June 1970.
15. Ibid.
16. *Irish Times*, 24–6 February, 3 & 13 March 1971.
17. *Irish Press*, 27 May 1971.
18. *Irish Press*, 1 June 1971.
19. *Anglo-Celt*, 3 December 1971.

# Author's Notes and Acknowledgements

My interest in the Ballinamore Canal grew out of an earlier investigation of the railway which served much the same region, and it was fuelled by a reading of what little there was in print concerning the waterway. The real stimulus behind the present project, however, came from the Very Rev F. J. McKiernan, the editor of *Breifne*, the excellent journal of Cumann Seanchais Bhreifne (Breifne Historical Society). He was kind enough to ask me to contribute an article on the canal to the journal—an essay which eventually ran to a rather excessive length—and his help was absolutely invaluable. In addition he introduced me to various people whose knowledge of the canal was matched only by their hospitality. I am most grateful to him and to the many people who helped me.

I am greatly indebted to Mr Paddy Quinn and to Mr John Edwards, who patiently answered my many questions and entertained me royally; to the Rev D. Gallogly, his brother, Joe, and his father, for their company on field trips, their hospitality, and their continued interest in my researches; to Professor and Mrs H. M. Power for their great assistance; to Dr D. B. McNeill, who gave me much help, particularly with the early references; to my brothers, Francis and John, for providing transport and company on field surveys; and to my parents for their great encouragement.

Thanks are also due to Messrs A. L. Dowley and W. Levinge,

and to Mr Charles Hadfield, who advised me throughout the
writing of this book. I extend my thanks to many other individuals too numerous to mention and whose assistance is greatly
appreciated. As much of my research was done in official
archives I owe of course a great debt to those who helped me
in this respect. I thank the staff of the National Library of Ireland who unfailingly came up with mountains of newspapers
and parliamentary records for study, and also the staff of the
Public Record Office of Ireland who equally willingly produced
even greater volumes of material. I thank Miss M. Griffith, the
Deputy Keeper of the Records, for permission to reproduce
figure 5 from the records in her care, and the National Library
for figures 1, 3, 4, 6, 7, 8. Mr Dick Mooney of the library's
photographic department provided some excellent microfilm of
old material. For invaluable help in the production of the half-
tone originals I am indebted to Mr Herbert Richards, who
made the final prints for me. The maps are based on the one-
inch series of the Ordnance Survey, and are reproduced by permission of the Government of the Republic of Ireland (Permit
No 1718). I am grateful for the assistance of the Deputy Assistant
Director of the Ordnance Survey Office.

Almost the last stage in the work was the production of a
satisfactory text for the publisher and in this respect I am indebted to Joan McManus, who expertly typed the final version.
In addition, she and her husband, Derry, were most generous
in their hospitality and they offered many constructive and
encouraging suggestions. I owe them both sincere thanks.

# Gazetteer of the Canal

BELOW is given a brief description—with a condensed history —of each of the engineering features along the canal. To aid in their location mileages are given on the left. The distances are reasonably precise, although the total length of the canal comes to only 36 miles. The official mileage of 38 miles 46 chains was arrived at taking into account 'the sailing course through the lakes', the precise details of which are now unknown. Many of the sites listed are very inaccessible and at some, for example Aghoo or Ardrum, it would be necessary to approach from both sides of the canal if a thorough inspection were to be made. Features are described as being on the left-hand (LH) or right-hand (RH) side of the canal as one moves along it from the Erne to the Shannon.

m.f.
- 0.0   *Upper Lough Erne.* Navigation begins at the junction of the parishes of Galloon, Kinawley and Drumlane.
- 0.3   Drumard Lough outfall (LH).
- 0.5   Anoneen Lough outfall (LH).
- 1.7   Corraback Lough outfall (LH).
- 2.7   *Aghalane Bridge.* Three-arch masonry structure built in 1848–9 to replace an earlier inadequate structure. Limited headroom in times of big floods.
- 4.5   *Caroul.* The waterway splits, the right-hand being the navigation channel on which is Lock No 1. Although it was built in 1849 the gates were not fitted till 1852; sluice gear was fitted in 1856. As with all the locks there have long been no gates. The left-hand channel curves around to a weir (built 1852–3) which had a fish pass and a large sluice for the discharge of

flood waters (fitted 1856). The latter no longer exists and the weir itself is badly broken. On the island between the channels was a two-storey toll collector's house built in 1857. Little trace of it remains. A footway used to lead from the house across the weir to the large sluice and on to the LH bank. There is now a rough bridge joining the island to the 'mainland' across the upper end of the lock.

5.5   Here begins a new navigation cut, some ¼ mile long, the old channel being on the left.

6.1   Navigation enters Cloncoohy Lough (old channel on LH) and then a new navigation cut, ½ mile long.

6.3   *Cloncoohy Bridge.* The original 1855 bridge was a 3-span timber structure which became quite infamous in later years. The present single-span concrete structure dates from c 1950.

7.3   *Ballyconnell Mill.* The mill is a little distance away (RH) and to the north of it the tail-race joins the waterway. Opposite the mill the channel divides, the old river course being on the left. The navigation channel almost immediately comes to Ballyconnell Lock (No 2; built 1849, fitted with gates 1852 and with sluice gearing 1855). Because of the mill the water level is maintained by a steel sluice gate erected in 1914 at the upper end of the lock. Opposite the other end of the lock (RH) is the lock-house, a small (21ft × 36ft approx) single-storey structure built in 1857 which is the only one of six still extant. Just past the lock (LH) is a water intake which fed two small turbines which provided electric current for the mill from around 1940. Nearly opposite this the headrace leaves the navigation channel. The only feature in the river channel (which curves around through Ballyconnell Demesne) was an eel fishery with a set of regulating sluices erected in 1852 as compensation for the removal of an older fishery. The stone piers which are all that remain of the fishery have been wrongly described as part of a flash lock.

7.6   *Ballyconnell Weir.* The weir is to the left of the navigation channel and at its near end are a large sluice and a fish pass. The former is the only such sluice to be found on the canal and it dates from 1931. Its continued existence is due to the mill; for the same reason the fish pass was repaired in 1932. The weir itself was built in 1849–50 and was completed by the erection of the original large sluice in 1856.

8.0   *Ballyconnell Quay and Bridge.* The former is on the right, just short of the bridge. About 120ft long it was provided with

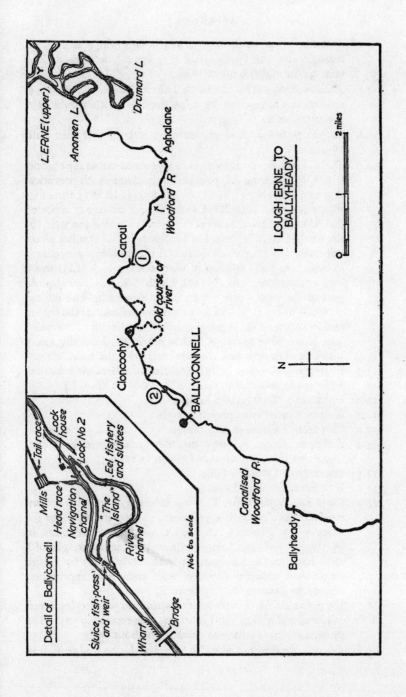

LERNE (upper)

Anoneen L.

Drumard L.

Aghalane

Woodford R.

Caroul

①

Old course of river

Cloncoohy

②

BALLYCONNELL

N

Canalised Woodford R.

Ballyheady

**Detail of Ballyconnell**

Mills
Tail race
Lock house
Head race
Lock No 2
Navigation channel
"The Island"
Eel fishery and sluices
River channel
Sluice, fish-pass and weir
Wharf
Bridge

Not to scale

**1 LOUGH ERNE TO BALLYHEADY**

0          1          2 miles

mooring posts when built in 1850. The bridge is a 2-arch masonry structure (with a smaller towpath—or 'horsewalk'— arch on the right) built in 1849.

8.3 *Railway Bridge*. The Cavan & Leitrim Railway (1887–1959) crossed the navigation by a low bridge which would have hindered boats.

10.6 *Ballyheady Bridge*. A single masonry arch of 45ft span built 1851–2.

12.7 *Skelan.* Here, from left to right, were ranged across the channel a lock, large sluice, fish pass and weir. After much prevarication the lock (No 3) was built in 1854–5. In 1855 the other structures were completed and of the weir it was reported that 'timber to raise the level of the water behind the weir, for the navigation to Aghoo, has been put on'. As at other places the sluice has long since gone and the masonry generally is in none too good condition. Opposite the lock (LH) was a lock house (erected in 1857) of which little trace remains. As part of the works here a 'permanent footbridge and railing' were put up 'to serve as a foot road and to facilitate the raising and lowering of the regulating boards at the top of the weir'. The latter have vanished and a couple of decidedly shaky plank bridges now link the east bank with the weir.

13.3 Entrance to Coologe Lough. (All the lakes here were marked with 'guide posts' or navigation 'beacons' in 1857–8.)

14.0 Entrance to Derrycassan Lough.

14.7 Entrance to Ballymagovern Lough.

15.2 Exit from Ballymagovern Lough.

15.4 *Ballinacor Bridge*. A single masonry arch erected by a contractor working for County Leitrim in 1854–5.

15.5 Entrance to Garadice Lake.

18.0 Exit from Garadice Lake.

18.2 *Carrickmakeegan Bridge*. This was originally a wooden accommodation bridge with a 35ft span, erected in 1855, but for many years a county road has crossed the canal here. In November 1968 the bridge collapsed under the weight of a sand lorry and it has been replaced (early 1971) by a high single-span concrete structure with embanked approaches, erected by Leitrim County Council.

18.7 *Derrygoan Bridge*. A wooden 35ft span bridge, carrying a 12ft roadway and giving 13ft headroom, was erected in 1855. The present concrete structure dates from about 1920.

19.2 *Lisnatullagh Bridge*. A wooden accommodation bridge with an

8ft roadway was erected in 1857. In later years the bridge was in such bad condition that the affected landowners had recourse to legal action. The present structure is an extremely ramshackle timber affair, supported by a concrete 'wall' in mid-channel and offering virtually zero headroom.

20.0 *Aghoo (Riversdale)*. Here, as at Skelan, are a lock, sluice, fish pass and 128ft weir. To the left is No 4 lock, built in 1854–5, and parallel to which was a lock house, built in 1857, of which little trace remains. The other works were built in 1854–5 and the large sluice was fitted up in 1856. Scanty remains still exist of the deep gates of the lock. The masonry generally is in poor shape.

20.2 *Aghoo Bridge*. A single-span masonry bridge, 35ft span by 21ft roadway, built in 1852–3.

20.7 *Railway Bridge*. Another crossing of the canal by the C & LR.

21.6 *Ardrum*. Features here were virtually identical to Skelan and Aghoo, and the arrangement was the same. The lock—No 5 —was built in 1851–2 and fitted with sluice gear in 1855. The 150ft long weir was built in 1852 and got its large sluice in 1856. There was no lock house. The masonry here is generally in fair condition.

22.2 *Ballinamore*. Just short of the town the channel divides. To the right is the old river course which swings left under a 3-arch bridge. Prior to the building of the C & LR in 1887 there was a quay (RH), similar to that at Ballyconnell, which was most conveniently placed near the Market House (1847–1971). The railway works were built on the site of this quay and they also obliterated the fourth arch of the river bridge. There is quite an expanse of water here—the 'basin'—which could handle pleasure boats easily although over the years its condition has been decidedly insanitary at times.

The navigation channel swings left, too, under a single arch stone bridge (built 1848–9) which has a towpath underneath (LH). On the northern side of the roadway between the navigation and river bridges was the lock house, built in 1857. Now demolished it was inhabited up to recent years. Ballinamore Lock (No 6) is some 200 yards from the bridge. It was built in 1849–50, fitted with gates in 1851–2 and given sluice gear in 1855. Its masonry is now in very bad condition and collapse of portions of it do not seem unlikely. Beyond the lock (RH) were, in order, the large sluice, fish pass and weir. The weir was built in 1850, the sluice fitted in 1856 and

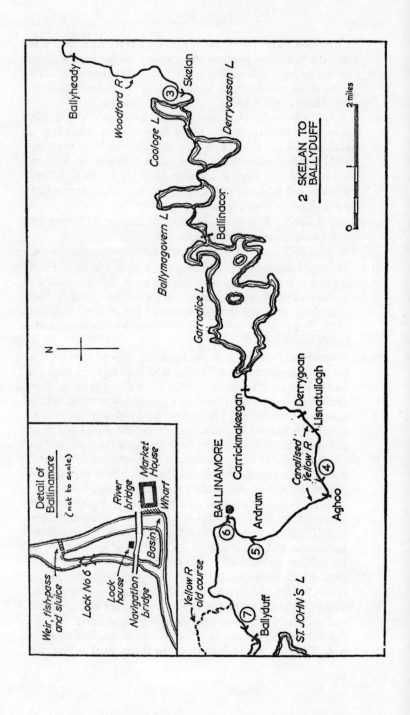

Detail of Ballinamore
(not to scale)

Weir, fish-pass and sluice
Lock No 6
Lock house
River bridge
Navigation bridge
Market House
Basin
Wharf

N

Ballyheady
Woodford R
Coologe L
Skelan
③
Derrycassan L
Ballymagovern L
Ballinacor
Garradice L

Carrickmakeegan
Derrygoan
Lisnatullagh
BALLINAMORE
⑥
Ardrum
Canalised Yellow R
⑤
④
Aghoo
Yellow R old course
⑦
Ballyduff
ST. JOHN'S L

2 SKELAN TO BALLYDUFF

0        2 miles

the fish pass—an after-thought—added in 1859. The site is now very heavily overgrown.

24.0 Junction (RH) with old course of Yellow River (diverted into St John's Lake).

24.4 *Ballyduff*. Once again, lock, sluice, fish pass and weir stretched across the channel, left to right. The lock (No 7) was built in 1853-4 and its sluices fixed up in 1855. The weir, 11ft high and 100ft long (with a dog-leg along it) was built and fully fitted in 1854. As at Skelan boards were fitted here to raise the level back to Castlefore. Masonry generally is quite sound.

24.5 *Ballyduff Bridge*. Single arch stone bridge, built 1849-50, with towpath underneath (LH).

24.7 Entrance to St John's Lough (also marked in 1857-8).

25.2 *Derrymacoffin Bridge*. A 35ft span accommodation bridge was erected here across narrows in the St John's lake system in 1854-5. A replacement bridge was provided in 1932 and collapsed in 1948 as two men and a horse and cart were crossing. The present concrete structure was put up shortly afterwards.

26.5 Muckros—exit from St John's Lough.

26.7 *Derrinkip Bridge*. A wooden accommodation bridge was built in 1855 and replaced in 1876. The present bridge is a more recent structure, consisting of a single narrow concrete span.

27.7 *Drumany Bridge*. This accommodation bridge, built in 1849, is one of the most interesting, being the only wrought iron lattice girder structure. It is narrow and rests on masonry abutments.

28.0 *Castlefore*. [Start of Summit Level.] The channel divides, navigation to the left where it immediately enters a lock, No 8, which was designed with a lift of no less than 13½ft. It was built in 1853-4 and fitted fully in 1855. It is now in poor condition. At its lower end (LH) was a lock house—also built in 1857 and now demolished. The right-hand channel runs parallel to the navigation one for some 300 yards to the weir, at the point where Aghacashlaun River used to flow in before its diversion into Lough Scur. The 100ft long weir was built in 1852-3 and finally completed with sluice in 1856. The fish pass was not added until 1859. This site is also heavily overgrown.

28.3 *Castlefore Bridge*. A masonry bridge with a single skew arch, built in 1851-2.

28.5 Entrance to Lough Marrave, a small lake ¼ mile long.

I

29.2    Entrance to Lough Scur. This lake is the central point of the summit level and it is fed by the diverted Kiltubrid (or Driney) and Aghacashlaun Rivers. It also had navigation markers.

30.6    Exit from Lough Scur.

31.2    *Lough Scur* (*Letterfine*) *Bridge*. This now carries a county road. It is a single masonry arch erected in 1852 as an accommodation bridge. The drainage award describes it as a public road bridge (Appendix 4).

31.4    *Letterfine Bridge*. A one-arch masonry bridge built in 1852. Both these bridges cross the deep rock cutting, the heaviest work on the canal.

32.1    *Scrabbagh Bridge*. An accommodation bridge, consisting of a masonry arch, built in 1850.

32.3    *Kilclare Bridge*. A very fine stone bridge, with towpath underneath its single skew arch (LH). Built 1849–50.

32.5    *Kilclare, Lock No 9*. [End of Summit Level.] This is the first of the 8 locks in the still-water canal section, all of which were built between 1849 and 1851 and which were fitted with gates in 1853, footboards, handrails etc in 1854, and sluice lifting gear in 1855. It is a fine lock with its masonry in quite good repair.

32.6    *Kilclare, Lock No 10*. This lock also has its masonry in quite good condition although bushes have encroached on it. An accommodation bridge across the lower end of the lock was provided 'for Mr King's tenants' in 1857. At present there is a concrete span across the lock. The ruins of Kilclare corn-mill are on the left.

32.7    *Kilclare, Lock No 11*. A very fine lock, still in good condition.

33.3    *Lisconor*. Just short of Lisconor Bridge (a slightly skewed arch, erected in 1849–50) is Lock No 12, also in reasonable condition although overgrown. To the right of the lock was a lock house, long since gone, which, however, did not have a resident lock keeper for long (see Appendix 3). It was built in 1857.

33.7    *Newbrook Lock, No 13*. A deep lock, in good repair but, like all others, without gates or sluices. It had an overflow drain (LH).

34.0    *Newbrook Bridge*. A stone structure with a skew arch and a towpath underneath (LH), this bridge was built in 1849–50.

34.1    *Sheffield*. This lock—No 14—also had an accommodation bridge built across its lower end (in 1859, for John Kane).

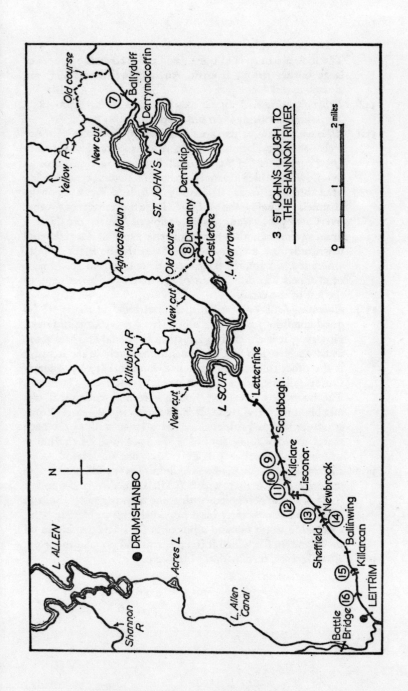

3 ST JOHN'S LOUGH TO THE SHANNON RIVER

N

L. ALLEN

DRUMSHANBO

Acres L.

Shannon R.

L. Allen Canal

Battle Bridge

⑯ Killarcan

⑮ Ballinwing

LEITRIM

Sheffield ⑬ ⑭ Newbrook

⑫ Lisconor

⑪ ⑩ ⑨ Kilclare

Scrabbagh

Letterfine

L. SCUR

New cut

Kiltubrid R.

New cut  Old course

L. Marrave

Castlefore

⑧ Drumany  Derrinkip

Aghacashlaun R.

ST. JOHN'S L.

Yellow R.

New cut

Old course

⑦ Ballyduff

Derrymacoffin

2 miles

0      1

The present bridge is a simple concrete span erected in 1926. The lock masonry is in quite good order though a couple of large bushes sprout from it. An overflow drain (LH) ran alongside this lock.

**34.6** *Ballinwing Bridge.* A single masonry arch dating from 1849. 'Crossycarwill Bridge' on OS Maps.

**35.1** *Killarcan.* A few yards short of Killarcan Bridge (a masonry arch—accommodation—built in 1850) is Lock No 15, also in good condition. On the left of the lock are the remains of an overflow by which drainage water fell *into* the canal having been brought from Ballinwing townland by a drainage channel. Just below the bridge (LH) are the remains of another overflow by which surplus water flowed *from* the canal into a drain which ran through Tirmactiernan and Carrickaveril townlands to a swampy region, formerly the Black Lough, where it again entered the canal, below Lock No 16. A maze of channels was dug as part of the drainage district here, to the left of the canal.

**35.4** *Killarcan, Lock No 16.* This, the last lock on the canal (in good condition) is occasionally referred to as 'Leitrim Lock'. However, it is situated in Killarcan townland and was more usually referred to by that name. Immediately to the left of it is the other toll collector's house, built in 1857 by Andrew Curley (all the other houses were by Matthew Gardiner). The house is still extant, though becoming ruinous; it was inhabited until the 1950s. It is a substantial two-storey stone structure with a yard, enclosed by a stone wall, at the back and a distinguishing feature is the back wall of the house which is completely blank, apart from one small window.

**35.7** *Leitrim.* The bridge here was built in 1849–50 and has a single masonry arch with towpath (LH). Immediately beyond it (LH) is a quay, complete with stone mooring posts, built in 1850. This has recently been provided with an electric light, a drinking water tap and a litter bin for boats coming in off the Shannon, for which it is a pleasant and popular mooring.

**36.1** *River Shannon,* termination of the canal.

# APPENDIX 2

# Ballinamore & Ballyconnell Navigation Trustees

AVAILABLE records are very scanty, and it is not possible to compile a list of guaranteed accuracy. The following list shows trustees known to have been appointed to office, irrespective of whether or not they were active. Conjectural dates are indicated. For some 15 years after 1878 the only trustees were nominal appointees or those who had been on the board prior to 1878 and had not died or resigned. County Roscommon authorities never appointed trustees; the only representatives for that county were appointed by the act 19 & 20 Vic, c 62.

*County Cavan*

| Period of Office | Name | Period of Office | Name |
|---|---|---|---|
| 1856 –1906? | Godley, Archibald | 1906?–1937 | McGovern, Francis |
| 1856 – ? | Johnston, Capt John | 1913 –1921 | O'Kane, John |
| 1856 – ? | Thornton, Perrott | 1913 –1929 | O'Reilly, Edward |
| ? –1887? | Vernon, John | 1922 –1937 | McAllister, Thomas |
| 1865?–1875? | Benison, James | 1930 –1937 | O'Reilly, Hugh |
| 1894?–1912 | Roe, S. B. | 1947 –1948 | Blake, C. J. |
| 1900?–1913 | O'Reilly, Thomas | 1947 –1948 | Davey, Crosbie |
| | | 1947 –1948 | Duffy, Francis |

## County Fermanagh

| Period of Office | Name | Period of Office | Name |
|---|---|---|---|
| 1856 –c1875 | Collins, Robert | 1894?–1939? | Porter, J. Porter |
| 1856 – 1885? | Erne, Earl of | 1919 –1937 | Benison, John A. |
| 1856 – 1873 | Porter, Rev J. G. | 1928 –1937 | Kiernan, Patrick |
| 1873 – 1878? | Porter, J. G. V. | 1940 –1948 | Carson, J. Nixon |
| 1878?– 1894? | Bailey, Major | 1940 –1948 | Enniskillen, Earl of |
| c1878?– 1919 | Irwin, John A. | 1940 –1948 | Porter, H. Archdale |
| 1894?– 1923? | Massy-Beresford, G. | | |

## County Leitrim

| Period of Office | Name | Period of Office | Name |
|---|---|---|---|
| 1856 –1897? | Latouche, Francis | 1900 –1920? | Kiernan, James A. |
| 1856 –1876 | Lawder, William | 1913 –1920? | O'Rourke, James |
| 1856 –1880? | O'Beirne, Hugh | 1924 –1937 | Mooney, Andrew |
| 1876 –1881 | Lawder, Rev Matthew | 1924 –1937 | O'Beirne, T. Rice |
| 1880?–1892? | Leitrim, Earl of | 1924 –1937 | Quinn, Francis |
| 1881?–1912 | Stewart, George | 1947 –1948 | Casey, Thomas |
| 1893?–1900? | Vaugh, Wilton | 1947 –1948 | Geoghegan, P. J. |
| 1900?–1920? | Keane, Bernard | 1947 –1948 | Pope, Charles J. |

## County Roscommon

| Period of Office | Name | Period of Office | Name |
|---|---|---|---|
| 1856– a | Kerkwood, James | 1856–1878 | Tenison, Edward King |
| 1856–1869 | Lorton, Viscount | | |

a James Kirkwood, JP, DL, of Woodbrook, Boyle, Co Roscommon, was almost certainly the 'Kerkwood' of the Act 19 & 20 Vic, c 62. He died in June 1857 and was not replaced, explaining why the Commissioners of Public Works could only correspond with two Roscommon trustees in 1860. The final dates in office for the latter are those of their deaths as it is not known if they were active.

# APPENDIX 3

# Employees of the Navigation

*Engineer*

| Name | Term of Office | Remarks |
|---|---|---|
| Pratt, James Butler | 6.1860– 2.1886 | Also secretary. Died 1886 |
| Irwin, Joseph | 2.1886–12.1914 | Appointment confirmed 1895. Died 1914 |
| Edwards, Peter | 1.1915– 3.1937 | Died 1937 |

*Secretary*

| Name | Term of Office | Remarks |
|---|---|---|
| Pratt, James Butler | 6.1860 – 2.1886 | See above |
| Benison, John Joseph | 2.1886?–10.1894 | Acting secretary from 1886? |
| Harrison, B. St George | 10.1894 – 8.1900 | Resigned |
| Hunt, E. L. | 8.1900 – 8.1901 | Died 1901 |
| Netterfield, James | 8.1901 –10.1916 | Resigned |
| Prior, John | 10.1916 – 1934 | Died 1934 |
| Prior, Patrick | 1934 | Acting secretary for short period |
| Quinn, Patrick | 4.1934 – 2.1948 | In office to last meeting |

William Lawder, one of the original trustees, was their honorary secretary prior to Pratt's appointment in 1860.

*Auditor*

| Name | Term of Office | Remarks |
|------|----------------|---------|
| Prior, John | 1913?–10.1916 | Became secretary |
| McCormack, John | 10.1916 – 1935 | Died 1935 |
| Higgins, Joseph | 7.1935 – 1936 | |

*Lock Keepers*

| House | Name | Year's Pay | Terms of Office | Locks Attended |
|-------|------|-----------|-----------------|----------------|
| Caroul | Murray, James | £3 | 7.1860– 7.1861 | Caroul |
| | Rafter, James | £3 | 7.1861– 1867 | |
| | Mohan, Charles | £3 | 1868– c1880 | |
| | Mohan, Mary | £3 | c1880– 1.1883 | |
| Bally-connell | ?McKenna, Patrick | £3 | c9.1859–10.1860 | Ballyconnell |
| | Winters, John | £3 | 10.1860– 1868 | |
| | Gilleece, John | £3 | 1869– 1893 | |
| | Gilleece, Patrick | a | 1894– c1940 | |
| | Gilleece, William | a | c1940– c1942 | |
| Skelan | Fitzpatrick, Patrick | £3 | c4.1860– 1877 | Skelan |
| Aghoo | Reilly, Hugh | £3 | c12.1859– 1877 | Aghoo |
| Ballina-more | McPharlane, Cormac | £4 | c1.1859– 1861 | Ardrum, Ballinamore, Ballyduff |
| | Ferguson, Michael | £4 | 1862– 1877 | |
| Castlefore | Melia, Francis | £3 | c2.1859– 1877 | Castlefore |
| Lisconor | ? Gill, James | b | ?1860–short period | b |
| Killarcan (Leitrim) | Gill, Charles | £5 | c6.1859– 1877 | Kilclare (3 locks), Lisconor, Sheffield, Newbrook, Killarcan (2 locks) |

a  The Gilleece family tended the sluices at the lock and at the weir. Patrick Gilleece was apparently unpaid (although like all lock keepers he got a free house) until 1918. After his death, c 1940, his brother tended the sluices for about 2 years.
b  Although there was a lock house at Lisconor there was definitely no lock keeper except for, possibly, James Gill for a short time in 1860. What locks would have been attended from Lisconor is conjectural.

*Caretaker*

| Name | Term of Office | Remarks |
|------|----------------|---------|
| McManus, John | 7.1929–7.1930 | Caretaker at Caroul to prevent obstructions being caused, for one year only |

# APPENDIX 4

# Extracts from the Final Awards

(referring to works on the navigation only)

*Drainage Award, Schedule B 'giving a description of the several Works executed in the . . . District'.*

. . . The improvement of the channel of the Woodford River, from Lough Erne to Garadice Lough.

The rebuilding of Aghalane, Ballyconnell and Ballyheady Bridges (county works) and building an occupation bridge at Cloncoohy.

The excavation and formation of navigable channels or side cuts, and the building of regulating weirs and waste sluices and fish passes, and navigation locks at Caroul, Ballyconnell and Skelan . . .

. . . The formation of a new drainage and navigation channel from Garadice Lough to St John's Lough.

The rebuilding of the public road bridges at Derrygoan, Aghoo and Ballyduff, and undersetting Ballinamore Bridge (county works), and building a new navigation arch at Ballinamore.

Building new regulating weirs, with waste sluices and fish passes, and new navigation locks at Aghoo, Drumraine [Ardrum], Ballinamore and Ballyduff.

The purchase of the water power of the Ballinamore Mill, and the purchase and removal of the mill, sluices, machinery, etc.

The erection of occupation bridges at Carrickmakeegan and Lisnatullagh . . .

. . . The excavation of the shoals at Derrymacoffin and Muckros, into St John's Lough, and the formation of a new navigation and drainage channel from St John's Lough to Lough Scur.

The building of accommodation bridges at Derrymacoffin, Branra [Derrinkip] and Drumany, and a navigation arch at Castlefore.

146

The building of a regulating weir, with waste sluices and fish pass, and a navigation lock at Castlefore . . .

. . . The excavation and formation of a new navigable channel from Lough Scur to the Shannon at the town of Leitrim.

The purchase of the water power of Kilclare Corn Mill.

The building of public road bridges at Lough Scur, Letterfine, Kilclare, Lisconor, Newbrook and Leitrim; and the building of occupation bridges in Scrabbagh, Drumruckill [Kilclare], Sheffield and Killarcan . . .

. . . The diversion of the Keonbrook and Ballinwing Streams into the canal [at Lock No 15], and the discharge of the surplus water at at overfall near Killarcan Bridge.

The deepening and improvement of the stream from the overflow at Killarcan Bridge . . . and diverting [it] into the canal below Lock No 15 [*recto* No 16].

The formation of a towing path from Garadice Lough to the Shannon, with fencing and horse bridges.

The building of Collectors' houses at Caroul and Killarcan, and of Lock Keepers' houses at Ballyconnell, Skelan, Aghoo, Ballinamore, Castlefore and Lisconor.

The erection of Guide Posts in Coologe Lough, Ballymagauran [Ballymagovern] Lough, Garadice Lough, St John's Lough and Lough Scur.

The building of trade wharves . . . at Ballyconnell, Ballinamore and Leitrim.

*Drainage Award, Schedule B[A] 'showing the portions of the foregoing works, for maintenance whereof, as works of Drainage, Trustees are to be appointed under the Act 5 & 6 Vict, c 89, and the Acts amending the same.'*

. . . The Cloncoohy occupation bridge . . .

. . . The occupation bridges in Carrickmakeegan and Lisnatullagh . . .

. . . The occupation bridges at Derrymacoffin, Branra [Derrinkip] and Drumany . . .

. . . The Scrabbagh, Drumruckill [Kilclare], Sheffield [Ballinwing] and Killarcan occupation bridges . . .

*Navigation Award, Schedule B specifying 'the works . . . the maintenance whereof as works of navigation is to be vested in and undertaken by the Ballinamore and Ballyconnell Navigation Trustees appointed under and by virtue of the Act 19 & 20 Vict, c 62'.*

The navigation channel from Lough Erne to the River Shannon; 15 [*recto* 16] navigation locks, length of chamber from recess to recess 82 feet, width between the uprights 16 feet 6 inches, and the depth of water on the sills 5 feet 6 inches; 8 regulating weirs, with waste sluices and fish passes; the overflow near Killarcan Bridge; the wharves at Ballyconnell, Ballinamore and Leitrim, and the approaches thereto; the navigation bridges at Ballinamore, Castlefore, Scrabbagh [Kilclare], Drumruckill [Lisconor], Sheffield [Newbrook], Killarcan [Ballinwing] and Leitrim; the Collectors' and Lock Keepers' houses; the guide posts through the lakes; the towing path, fences and bridges.

Note: The alternative names given in brackets are those by which the features in question are referred to in the text and especially in Appendix 1. In most cases both names are equally correct as the navigation largely runs along townland boundaries but in some instances the names are very loosely if not wrongly used above. For instance, there is no public road bridge in Drumruckill townland. The bridge in question is on the boundary between the townlands of Lisconor and Kilclarebeg and is referred to as Lisconor bridge. In view of the glaring inconsistencies between the terminologies of the two awards it is not in the least surprising that the trustees became confused at times. There is only one bridge in the townland of Killarcan yet the above implies that an occupation bridge and a navigation bridge were built in the townland. Of two identical bridges there is reason to believe that the latter is the bridge linking the townlands of Sheffield and Ballinwing and referred to by the latter name. The problems could have been solved by the official maps which accompanied the awards but which have not survived.

# Index

Figures in *italic* refer to illustrations